Out
of
China's
Earth

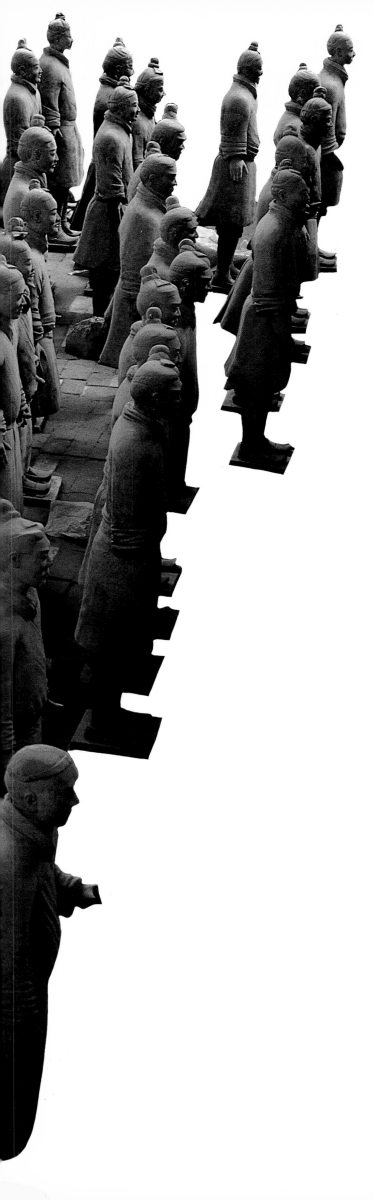

Out
of
China's
Earth

Archeological
Discoveries
in the
People's Republic
of China

Qian Hao,
Chen Heyi, and Ru Suichu

Harry N. Abrams, Inc.

Publishers, New York

and

China Pictorial, Beijing

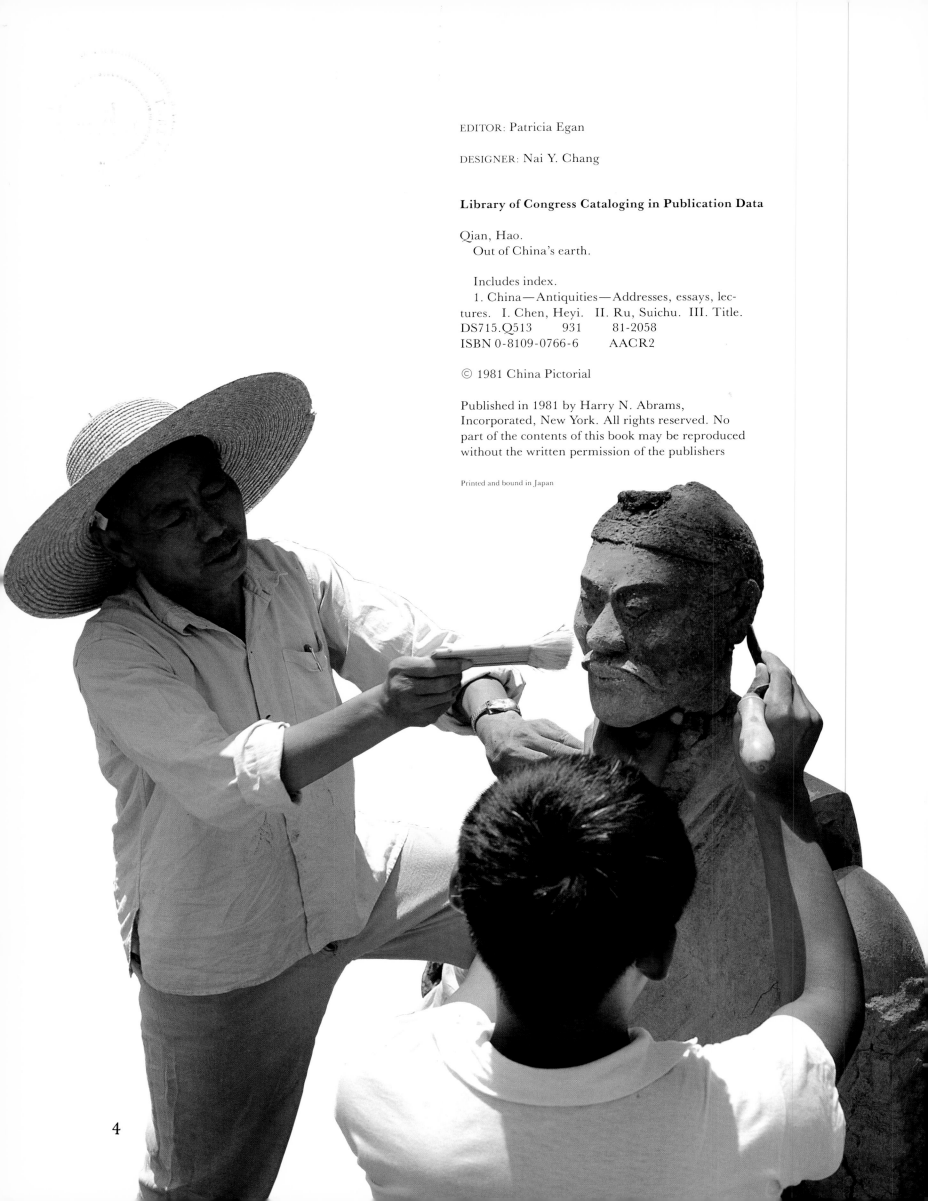

EDITOR: Patricia Egan

DESIGNER: Nai Y. Chang

Library of Congress Cataloging in Publication Data

Qian, Hao.
    Out of China's earth.

    Includes index.
    1. China—Antiquities—Addresses, essays, lec-
tures. I. Chen, Heyi. II. Ru, Suichu. III. Title.
DS715.Q513   931   81-2058
ISBN 0-8109-0766-6   AACR2

4

Contents

Preface

This book is about cultural objects that have been excavated from China's earth since 1949, the year of the founding of the People's Republic of China. It is an illustrated record of only the most characteristic cultural relics, those having an artistic and historical interest that will appeal widely to readers everywhere. Accident brought about their discovery, in many instances; after they were dug up, they were cleaned and restored to as near their original appearance as possible.

China is among the most ancient countries, and has made glorious gifts to mankind. Like the ancient cultures of Egypt, Mesopotamia, and India, which developed along great rivers, the ancient civilization of China was nurtured by the earth along the banks of the Changjiang and Huang He rivers. Myth and legend veils the beginning of Chinese history some 5,000 years ago. The earliest known Chinese characters, those in the oracle inscriptions on bone and tortoiseshell, take us back some 3,000 years. The cultural relics left by these Chinese ancestors span a long time—from Shang-Yin and Zhou to Qin and Han, and down the successive dynasties. The relics have been found over an extended range—from Heilongjiang in the north to the Sisha Islands in the south, and from Xinjiang in the west to Taiwan in the east.

Certain relics survived the ages aboveground; among these are palaces, citadels, grottos, temples, and monasteries, and sculpture, murals, and pagodas. The most representative are the Great Wall that meanders among folds of mountains in the north, and the magnificent imperial palace in Beijing. The relics dug from underground include very numerous stone and jade objects, silks, pottery and lacquerware, bronze vessels and articles of gold and silver, documents, ancient writings, and tomb paintings. All together they form a kaleidoscope of Chinese cultural life.

The ten chapters in this book have been selected with care; from Shang-Yin in the fourteenth century B.C. to the Tang Dynasty in the tenth century A.D., they cover much of the slave society and the flourishing feudal society, a span of more than 2,000 years. Among the objects are the mighty Shang Dynasty bronzes recently unearthed from the Fu Hao tomb in the Yin

Ruins, and the later bronze "Flying Horse" which was recently exhibited in many countries. The colorful silks miraculously preserved in the Mawangdui tombs give us a glimpse of the high level of the silk industry at an early time. We see the ancients' predilection for jade, as well as the jade carvers' expertise, in the carved jade figures of the Shang-Yin period and the Western Han nobles' jade burial suits tied with gold thread. Ancient musical instruments, such as the bronze bells and stone-chimes, the flutes, pipes, and zithers, provide data for rewriting that area of the history of music. The silk paintings in the Mawangdui tombs demonstrate the ancient artists' skill, and the silk books and maps are very important documents, the first of their kind. The lifesize terracotta soldiers and horses, part of the mausoleum of the First Emperor of Qin, have been acclaimed an eighth wonder of the world.

It is no exaggeration to say that among these cultural relics there are rare treasures. Excavations are still going on, and more will be brought to light. The discovery of these sites and graves has excited the interest and attention of people everywhere, scholars and public alike. Questions raised and answered by the cultural relics published here touch upon China's political and economic systems and its cultural, scientific, technical, and everyday life in ancient times, and what these can mean to the world today.

All works illustrated in this chapter are
in the Chinese Museum of History,
Beijing, unless otherwise indicated

1. *Si gong*, wine container in the shape of
a cow, hind legs those of a bird.
Height 14 1/4″, length 18 1/4″

1. The Yin Ruins and the Tomb of Fu Hao

China's Earliest Dynastic Capital

China's recorded history begins with the Shang Dynasty.

The Xia Dynasty (c. 21st century B.C.–c. 16th century B.C.), Shang Dynasty (c.16th century B.C.–11th century B.C.), and Western Zhou Dynasty (c.11th century B.C.–771 B.C.) are frequently mentioned in ancient Chinese historical texts. The historical limits of Xia, the earliest, have never been determined and its beginnings are known only through legend. One of the most famous legends tells of how Yu the Great, the first Xia ruler, tamed a great flood. Recent excavations, however, have provided archeologists and historians with a clue to guide them in their search for remains of the Xia culture.

As for Shang culture, we are now able to form a clearer picture of it with the aid of large numbers of excavated "oracle inscriptions," as well as bronzes, jade and stone carvings, and other relics.

According to an ancient Chinese historian, the Shang Dynasty was established after the overthrow of the Xia Dynasty, and reigned for about 600 years: its thirty-one kings spanned seventeen generations. In its early period, the Shang royal house successively occupied several seats, but during the fourteenth century B.C., King Pan Geng of the tenth generation established the Shang capital at Yin, near modern Anyang in Henan Province; he and his twelve successors remained in Yin for about 270 years, and this dynasty itself was also alternatively known as Yin after the capital had been moved there.

In 1899, peasants working in the fields of Xiaotun village in Anyang hit upon some tortoiseshells and animal bones bearing ancient inscriptions. These soon attracted attention, for they proved to be the first oracle inscriptions discovered in China. Investigations show that Xiaotun and its adjacent regions were occupying the ancient site of Yin, the Shang capital for the reigns of Pan Geng to Zhou, the last of the Shang kings. The site is now known as the Yin Ruins. Excavations at the Yin Ruins, especially those during the last thirty years, give us some idea of the Shang capital of Yin.

Anyang is located near a plain with the Huan River snaking

2. Aerial view of the Yin ruins in Anyang, Henan Province

3. Oracle inscription on bone

4. Oracle inscription on tortoiseshell. Exhibition Hall of the Yin Ruins, Anyang

5. Tomb No. 5 under excavation. In the background is the village of Xiaotun. Archeological Institute, Beijing

through it. The palace was centered on the south bank of the river, where the village of Xiaotun is today. Around the palace were commoners' settlements, handicraft workshops, and tombs. Farther out were workshops for making bronze and bone objects. On the north bank, in and around Wuguancun and Houjiazhuang villages, were royal tombs, tombs of the nobility, and sacrificial pits, surrounded by commoners' dwellings and graves. The site of the ancient capital covers an area of almost ten square miles.

The total number of oracle bones and shells removed from the Yin Ruins exceeds 100,000, for it was common practice among the Shang rulers to consult the oracle whenever in doubt. The diviners' questions and the responses of the oracle were written or inscribed on animal bones or tortoiseshells in pictographs—the earliest form of Chinese writing. The characters were not written on the oracle bones in any set form, but were sometimes in horizontal order, sometimes vertical; some read from left to right, others from right to left. Chinese writing was still primitive in form, yet the oracle bones and shells are of the utmost value for the study of the Shang Dynasty. Together with the large quantity of articles for everyday use—tools, weapons, and ornamental objects—and the excavated ruins of the palace and workshops, they tell us much about the brilliant Shang culture.

Tomb No. 5 at the Yin Ruins and Its Bronze and Jade Furnishings

In 1976 the Anyang archeological team of the Institute of Archeology discovered a well-preserved tomb near the ruins of

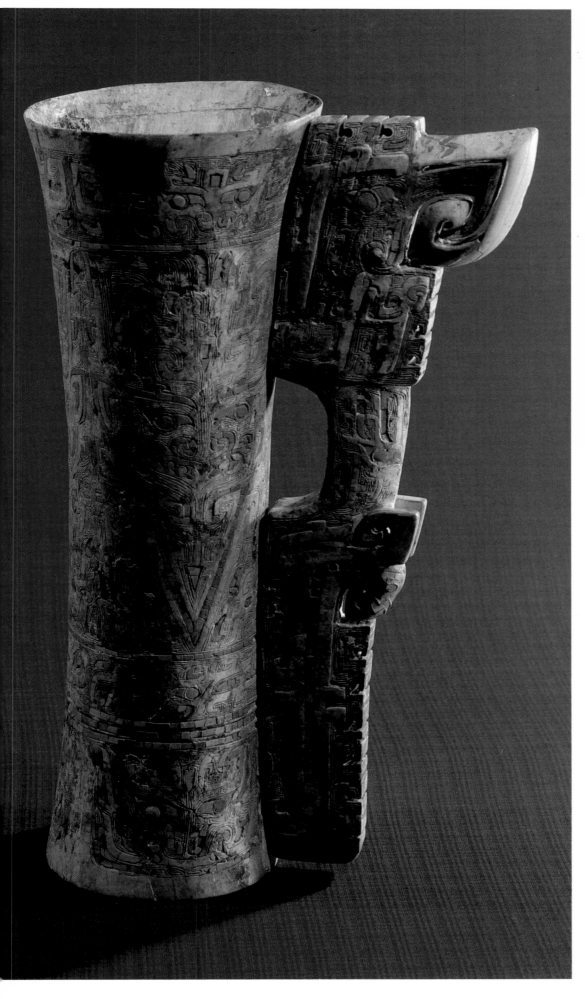

6. Ivory wine container with turquoise inlay. Height 11 7/8''

7. Stone cow. Length 9 3/4''

8. Stone cicada. Length 5 1/2''

9. Members of the Anyang archeological team examining bronzes excavated from Fu Hao tomb

10. Human sacrifices in a royal tomb. Slaves including men, women, and children were entombed with the deceased, some buried alive, others after decapitation

the Shang palace northwest of Xiaotun. It was designated Tomb No. 5.

The tomb is not important for its scale, which is modest, but for its undisturbed condition. The tomb chamber has yielded a great amount of tomb furniture, more than any of the other Shang royal tombs excavated at the Yin Ruins. Altogether, more than 1,600 articles have been brought to light, including 440 bronze vessels, weapons, and tools, 570 jade objects, and 560 bone artifacts. In addition, there are 7,000 cowrie shells (probably used as money), plus some stone sculptures, ivory carvings, and pottery.

According to the bronzes and oracle inscriptions, the tomb occupant was Fu Hao, one of the royal consorts of King Wu Ding of Shang. This is the only tomb thus far discovered at the Yin Ruins that can be clearly identified as to both its occupant and its date.

The tomb pit is an oblong shaft; skeletons of human and dog sacrifices were found in it, but the wooden chamber and its contents, the lacquer coffin and the skeleton of the occupant, have all disintegrated. The deceased was interred with no fewer than sixteen human sacrifices. These included men, women, and children, and at least one had been slaughtered before interment;

11. Rectangular *ding* on flattish dragon legs, cooking vessel. Earlier rectangular *ding* have round legs; flat legs are rare. Height 16 3/4″. Exhibition Hall of the Yin Ruins, Anyang

another was slashed at the waist and then buried. To bury slaves, either alive or after decapitation, with their deceased masters was a common practice in the slave society of Shang.

A Shang structure was built over the pit site, rectangular in shape and a bit larger than the mouth of the pit. Judging from similar instances in previous excavations of Shang tombs at the Yin Ruins, this surface building was most probably erected for the purpose of holding memorial ceremonies for the dead, or as a component part of a royal tomb.

The bronzes excavated here form the most complete group of their kind ever found intact in a Shang tomb at these ruins. They include ceremonial vessels, musical instruments, weapons, articles of everyday use, and objects of art. Many of them bear inscriptions.

Of the bronzes, a four-piece set of cooking vessels is the first of its kind ever discovered in China. The set consists of a rectangular cooking range and three *zeng* steamers, and weighs 248 pounds. Supported by six legs, the cooking range has three trumpet-mouthed sockets on its top with decorative designs on the rims. A coiling dragon surrounds each socket. The four corners of the range are adorned with ox-head motifs, and on the inside of the middle socket, near the mouth, are inscribed the

12. (*opposite*). Rectangular *ding*, a large cooking vessel, inscribed with the words "Si Mu Xin"—posthumous title conferred on the mother or queen of a Shang king. Height 31 1/2"; weight 258 lbs.

13. (*right*) Round *ding* of medium size. Height 11 5/8", diameter across mouth 10"; weight about 22 lbs.

14. (*below*) Round *ding*, cooking vessel. Height 23 3/8", diameter across mouth 21 1/2"; weight 111 lbs.

15. (*overleaf*) The triple *yan* steamer, a 4-piece cooking set consisting of a rectangular range and three steamers. Weight 248 lbs.; length 40 1/2", width 10 1/2", height 17 1/2". The legs are 7 1/2" high; trumpet-like rims of the sockets are each 2 1/4" high and 7 3/4" across; steamers are 10 1/4" high, 13" across top, and 6" across bottom

16. Round *jia* goblet. Height 26 1/8″

17. Rectangular *jia* goblet, used
    exclusively for holding sacrificial wine.
    Height 27″

19. *Bu*, wine container. Height 13 1/2″

18. Twin owl-shaped *zun*, wine vessels. Height of each 18″

20. Casket-shaped twin *yi*, large wine container unprecedented in its form. The characters "Fu Hao" are inscribed on the inside bottom. Height 23 1/2″, length 34 3/4″

characters "Fu Hao." With soot stains still on its legs and bottom, the range was apparently in daily use. Each of the three steamers also bears the characters "Fu Hao" on the inside wall and on the outside of the two handles. Called by the name triple *yan* steamer, this range and many other bronzes, such as the *ding* cooking vessels, the *zun, hu, lei,* and *bu* wine containers, and the *gong* and *jia* wine goblets, all exquisitely executed and varied in shape and size, tell much about the luxurious life and extravagance of the Shang rulers.

The fine workmanship and the intricate designs of the bronzes unearthed from Tomb No. 5 are vivid evidence that China's bronze culture was already in its most prosperous era—the Shang–Zhou period. The size of the hoard also shows that bronzes were then being produced on a large scale.

Of the jade objects unearthed from the tomb, those of green jade are first in number, and brown jades second. The ceremonial articles include *cong* (hollow jade piece with rectangular sides), *bi* (round flat jade piece with a central hole), *huan* (ring), and *gui* (food container); weapons of jade carried by guards of honor, such as *ge* (dagger-ax), *mao* (spear), *yue* (ax), *dao* (sword), and *fu* (also ax). Many figurines, animals, and ornaments were found and a rare mortar and pestle for use in pounding cinnabar, the like of which has never been found before.

Jade objects were much prized in the Shang times. Information gleaned from the oracle inscriptions identifies jade articles used in important ritual services, and jade ornaments were

22. Two bronze mirrors, the oldest bronze mirrors thus far found in China. Diameter about 4 3/4"

23. *Yue,* bronze ax with inscription "Fu Hao." Height 15 1/2", length of blade about 14 1/2"; weight 19 1/2 lbs.

24. Jade *gui,* food container. Height 5", wall thickness 1/2"

25. Jade dagger-ax with bronze handle. Entire length 11", pointed blade 6 1/4". The handle is embellished with *taotie* (stylized animal face) designs and inlaid with turquoise.

26. Jade dagger-ax, length 14 1/4". Six delicate Chinese characters at the upper end signify: "a tribute of five dagger-axes"

27. Jade mortar and pestle. Height 10-1/2", diameter 6 1/4", depth 5 1/4", thickness of wall 3 1/4". The pestle is 11" long, 2 1/2" thick. Red stains show that this was to pound cinnabar

24

25

23

26

27

21. (*opposite*) *He,* a bronze vessel for diluting wine. Height 15 1/4"

28

29

30

31

common among the Shang aristocrats. Members of the aristocracy were usually buried with their most precious jade possessions, a practice which continued into succeeding dynasties. Eventually, burial garments made entirely of jade plaques tied together with gold thread were used in burial (see Chapter 6).

The jade objects uncovered from Tomb No. 5 are of fine workmanship, the ornaments and objects of art being particularly natural as well as beautiful in shape. They tell much about their creator's imagination. The figurines are vivid in expression, within succinct contours. They present a good picture of the life in Fu Hao's social stratum.

The jade animals and birds—coiled dragon, ready-to-leap tiger, crouching bear with raised head, elephant with lifted trunk, and long-tailed phoenix—each is unique and all are in some way true to life. One mythical creature combines some features of a bird with others of an animal.

These are the oldest existing jade treasures in China, and they attest to the high artistic level attained by the fine craftsmen in the Shang period.

Fu Hao, Principal Occupant of Tomb No. 5

The inscriptions on bronzes unearthed from the tomb prove that its occupant was Fu Hao.

28. (*opposite*) A human face mold, discovered at the Yin Ruins. 5 1/2 × 5″. The face resembles those of jade and stone figurines from Fu Hao tomb
29. Jade and stone figurines, with differing hair styles. Height 2 1/2″ to 3 1/4″
30. Jade dragon. Length 3 1/8″
31. Jade tiger. Length 4 1/2″

32. (*below*) Jade birds of fantastic shape combining a bird's body, animal's feet, and sheep's horns. They show the rich imagination of the carvers. Heights 2″ to 3″
33. Jade bear. Height 1 1/2″
34. Jade phoenix. Length 5 1/4″
35. Jade ornament with dragon and phoenix designs. Height 5 1/8″
36. Jade pigeon. Height 2″
37. Jade elephant. Length 2 1/2″
38. Jade eagle. Height 2 1/4″

The name Fu Hao, although not found in historical texts, appears often in oracle inscriptions dated within the reign of King Wu Ding of Shang. A search for the king's name in the 100,000 oracle inscriptions found in the Yin ruins reveals about 170 instances of it. King Wu Ding had sixty-four wives, but Fu Hao, one of these royal consorts, is mentioned more frequently and in connection with a wider scope of activities than others—Fu Geng, Fu Liang, Fu Shu, and Fu Zhu—and hers was evidently the more influential position.

Wu Ding, one of the famous Shang kings, was the fourth traditional king of the royal house occupying the new capital of Yin. During his reign of fifty-nine years, he chose men of ability to fill government posts, and he adopted a number of measures toward restoring the glory of Yin. To extend the influence of his kingdom, he made war against various tribes, conquering Hu Fang in the south, She Fang in the north, Qiang in the west, Yi in the east, and Be Ce in the southwest.

Oracle inscriptions show that Fu Hao had an important part in the king's war effort against Qiang. Qiang and Shang armies had often met in battle before, but Fu Hao was now in command of an army of 13,000. She also led an expedition against Tu Fang, a tribal state in the northwest. An oracle inscription reads: "The king has mastered his troops and is going to conduct a military campaign with Fu Hao as its commander against Tu Fang this year. Will he be protected?" Fu Hao also participated in the wars against Ba Fang in the southwest and Yi in the east. According to the oracle inscriptions, she was an able general under the bellicose King Wu Ding, and fought in the west, north, southwest, and east.

Shang belonged to the slave society, and it is characteristic that the Shang kings greatly revered their ancestors and their gods. Matters of ancestor worship and military affairs were of the utmost concern for the kingdom; except for the king himself, only persons in high position—the king's trusted followers or high-ranking officials—were qualified to command the army and to preside over sacrificial rites. Oracle inscriptions tell us that Fu Hao led military expeditions against external enemies and conducted ceremonies in worship of the Shang ancestors and the gods. In presiding over these ceremonies, she made offerings of wine, and prisoners of war, slaves, and cattle were sacrificed.

The oracle inscriptions and the fine burial objects found in her tomb confirm that Fu Hao was an important figure and a famous general in the reign of King Wu Ding. She died before the king did. Oracle inscriptions tell us that her death so saddened the king that he wept in grief while offering sacrifices to her and often dreamed of her in his sleep.

The Shang Culture

The tomb of Fu Hao is calculated to date from the first half of the twelfth century B.C.

Since the discovery of oracle inscriptions at Xiaotun in Anyang in 1899, the Yin Ruins have attracted the attention of historians and archeologists throughout the world. Chinese and foreign scholars agree that the finely wrought bronzes of the Shang Dynasty are historical evidence of the high level of that Chinese civilization. Ancient man required a long, long time to proceed from the stone and pottery cultures to extracting copper from ore. Copper and bronze objects—awls, chisels, knives, daggers, and rings—that date back to the Qijia culture, 2000 B.C., have been discovered in Gansu Province. By the time of the Shang, bronzes were produced in large numbers and the art of manufacturing them had already attained a high degree of perfection. In the 270 years and more after Yin became the Shang capital, the Shang Dynasty, now politically stable and powerful, made great progress in its economy and culture. The sites of bronze casting discovered at the Yin Ruins total about four square miles in area, with pottery sherds and bits of crucibles scattered all over it. The Houmuwu cauldron uncovered from the Yin ruins is over fifty-two inches high and weighs almost one ton; it is the largest ancient bronze found in China, or in the world. The many rare bronze treasures unearthed from Fu Hao's tomb add luster to the bronze culture of the Shang Dynasty.

Since the founding of New China in 1949, bronzes attributed to an earlier date than those at the Yin ruins have been discovered from Shang tombs in Zhengzhou, Henan Province. Indeed, Shang Dynasty bronzes have been found over a vast area, from eastern Liaoning Province in the north to south of the Changjiang River, and from Zhejiang Province in the east to Shaanxi and Gansu provinces in the west. This rich material shows that the sway of the Shang Dynasty was not confined to the three provinces of Henan, Shandong, and Hebei, as had been believed before these discoveries.

Shang society was already an agricultural one. Under the prevailing conditions of production, nature still dominated agriculture and animal husbandry. People believed that their destiny and the outcome of their crops were decided by the unseen gods. Superstitions governed the whole society; the rulers worshiped their gods and ancestral spirits, and consulted the oracle for guidance in their future activities. The beautiful bronze ware they used in their ceremonies or displayed in their ancestral temples represented the best bronze-casting technique of the time, and the shapes and decoration reflected the rulers' political and religious beliefs and aesthetic conceptions. Many of the decorations

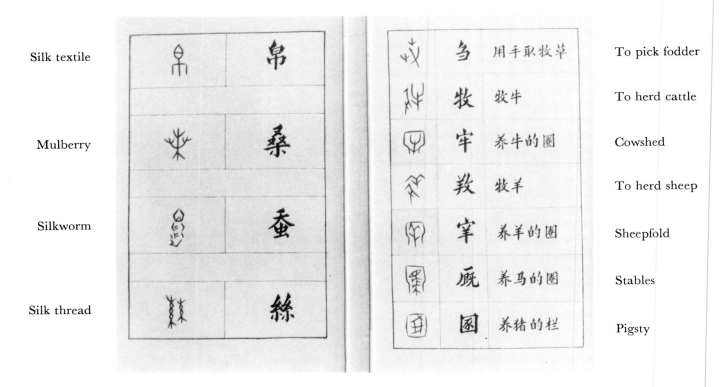

Silk textile	帛	用手取牧草	To pick fodder
		牧牛	To herd cattle
Mulberry	桑	养牛的圈	Cowshed
		牧羊	To herd sheep
Silkworm	蚕	养羊的圈	Sheepfold
		养马的圈	Stables
Silk thread	絲	养猪的栏	Pigsty

39. Shang oracle-bone characters relating to animal husbandry and silkworm breeding. Modern printed Chinese equivalents are on the right

are based on animals and natural phenomena, among these the thunder-and-cloud design and the spiral motif which represented fire. The creatures on the bronzes are not real animals, but are imaginary beasts for the most part, composed loosely and then elaborated and refined by the imagination of the casters. Among these are the phoenix (stylized bird), dragon (deified serpent), and *taotie* (stylized face of a man-eating beast). The various motifs signified royal authority, exorcism of evil spirits, or good luck. They lend a mysterious look to the austere Shang bronzes.

The Shang bronzes can be assigned to categories according to their uses: tools of production, weapons, cooking vessels, wine vessels, water containers, and chariots and harness. The wine vessels are greatly varied in shape and style, and are higher in artistic quality than most of the other vessels. This suggests that the Yin people were fond of drinking, and indeed King Zhou, the last Shang king, was reported in Sima Qian's *Historical Records* to have indulged in debauchery and wine. In his search for pleasure he built a wine reservoir in his garden, and hung meat on the trees surrounding it. By the late Shang period the rulers had amassed huge wealth through the exploitation of slaves, and led lives of luxury and extravagance.

Animal husbandry reached a fairly developed stage during the Shang Dynasty. The names of all the domestic animals we now know are found in the oracle inscriptions. For a single ritual ceremony or royal burial, hundreds of cattle and sheep might be sacrificed.

The main productive work in the Shang period, however, was farming. In the oracle inscriptions there are characters for rice seedlings, wheat, glutinous millet, and paddy rice; and for field, farmland, well, boundary, *mou* (Chinese land measure), and nursery. Also in the oracle vocabulary are words connected with the stone, jade, bone, and bronze industries (sites of which have been discovered at the Yin ruins), and other industries such as tanning, wine-making, ship-building, chariot-making, civil engineering, silkworm raising, brocade-weaving, and sewing. The large number of cowrie shells in Fu Hao's tomb indicates that cowries had a value that was sought after by the nobles, pointing to their probable use as currency in the economy of the time.

Shang was a slave society and agriculture, animal husbandry, and the handicraft industries were mostly accomplished by the slaves. The slaves, therefore, created these admirable bronze and jade treasures, the wealth of the society, and ultimately the culture of Shang.

2. The Long-forgotten State of Zhongshan and Its Cultural Relics

There are turbulent stretches in the long flow of history, and tiny drops may blow off from the waves of the rapids.

The State of Zhongshan, which existed more than 2,000 years ago, has long ceased to be remembered—and even the name of its most powerful ruler, King Cuo, is not to be found in China's historical texts. Thanks to our archeologists we now have some insight into this forgotten state—a drop of water lost for so long in the river of history.

Many of the relics from Zhongshan such as the gold- and silver-inlaid bronze base in the shape of a tiger devouring a deer and the bronze lamp-tree with fifteen oil cups would be art treasures in any age. They are finds from the tomb of a Zhongshan ruler in Lingshuo, the capital of Zhongshan. The tomb area is now in Pingshan County on the northern bank of the Hutuo River some 50 miles west of Shijiazhuang, capital of Hebei Province. Together with the art treasures, two liquids having an ambrosial aroma were brought to light. How had they remained fluid, unevaporated through more than 2,000 years? The question is intriguing and puzzling.

A State of the White Di

Long before Zhongshan there had lived two nomadic tribes called the Rong and the Di, or Yanyun, who roamed over northern China in search of pasture and water. They were close neighbors of the Huaxia people, the ancestors of the Hans who inhabited the Central Plain in the Huang He Valley, and one of the earliest civilized peoples in the world.

The Western Zhou Dynasty, established by the Huaxia people, began to decline during the ninth century B. C., while the vassal states under Zhou, also established by the Huaxia people, became steadily more powerful. In 771 B.C. the duke of the State of Shen killed King You of Zhou at the foot of Mount Lishan, in present-day Lintong in Shaanxi Province. The following year Yi Jiu, son of King You, was made king. He moved his capital eastward to Luoyang, thus marking the end of the Western Zhou Period and the beginning of what historians call the Eastern Zhou.

All works illustrated in this chapter are in the custody of the Cultural Relics Department, Hebei Province, Shijiazhuang

40. Head of tiger (see Plate 50)

41. Tomb No. 1 of Zhongshan in Pingshan County, Hebei Province. Fifty feet deep, it stretches 300 feet from east to west, 360 feet from north to south. King Cuo was buried there in about 310 B.C. It yielded many valuable bronzes

In the course of Eastern Zhou, the king became ruler of his country in name only, being unable to hold the kingdom together. The ducal states under him were constantly at war, each wanting to dominate the others. Taking advantage of this turmoil, the Di and the Rong tribes gradually entered the Central Plain.

During this period the White Di, a branch of the Di people, left their home in northern Shaanxi and moved eastward. Becoming a powerful political force in China by 662 B.C., the White Di founded a state in 530 B.C. by the name of Xianyu in the vicinity of present-day Shijiazhuang, in Hebei Province east of the Taihang Mountains, with Xinshixian (now Xinchengpu, twelve miles northeast of Zhengding County) as its capital.

Xianyu was conquered by the State of Chu between 515 B.C. and 510 B.C., but the ruler had managed to escape and soon staged a comeback. After regaining its territory Xianyu changed its name to Zhongshan and moved its capital to Gu (present-day Dingxian, Hebei Province). In the meantime the State of Jin, which bordered Zhongshan on the west, emerged as a strong power and swallowed up the small states of Fi and Gu, both also set up by the White Di; Zhongshan, however, remained unharmed. In 507 B.C. Jin attacked Zhongshan but was defeated at Pingzhong.

Due to wars of annexation among the dukedoms and marquisites, there remained by 403 B.C. only Qin, Qi, Wei, Han, and a few other larger states from the numerous former smaller ones. More wars were fought among these until finally Qin unified China in 221 B.C., ending the Warring States Period in the history of China.

In 408 B.C. the powerful Wei attacked Zhongshan, their neighbor on the north, and subjugated it. Twenty years later the Zhongshan nobles, who had refused to accept defeat, rose in arms in Huihe, vanquished the Wei troops, and recovered their lost territory.

Lingshuo became the capital of the reestablished Zhongshan, and here began its golden age. Zhongshan developed into a well-administered, prosperous, and powerful state having a thousand war chariots able to contend with the chief states for hegemony.[1] In the south Zhongshan defeated Zhao, a state of ten thousand war chariots, at Changzi; and it met Yan, another state of ten thousand war chariots, in battle at Zhongshan and killed Yan's commander. At this time, Zhongshan's territory extended as far as the foothills of the Taihang Mountains in the west; to Anping, Liangxian, Xinhe, and Julu in the east; to Anxin and Xushui in the north; and to Gaoyi in the south. The relics that have been uncovered at Pingshan probably belong to this period.

Until the recent excavations no one knew of the royal lineage of Zhongshan. It had not been mentioned in Chinese historical records, but a bronze inscription unearthed at Pingshan reveals that Zhongshan had five rulers during the Lingshuo period: in lineal orders, these were Duke Huan, Duke Cheng, King Cuo, Jie Zhi, and King Shang. Before the Wei occupation the last two rulers had been Duke Wen and Duke Wu. Another bronze inscription tells us that Zhongshan participated in 314 B.C. in the war waged by the State of Qi against Yan, and as a result seized from Yan "several hundred *li* of land and scores of cities and towns."

The Merging Nationalities

The State of Zhongshan was founded by White Di people but its culture, to judge from the tools of production found at Pingshan and the articles of jade and bronze, was very similar to that of the Central Plain.

According to historical records, Xianyu—predecessor of Zhongshan—was a land where the "fragrance of grain crops filled the air and farm cattle were seen grazing among horses." Xianyu was located close to an agricultural district in and around the capital of the Shang Dynasty (c. 16th century B.C.–c. 11th century) that was peopled by Shang descendants, and the White Di, through years of interchange with their Huaxia neighbors, had gradually become semi-nomadic and semi-agricultural. Xianyu

---

[1] Wars were fought with chariots in ancient China. War chariots were also used to transport military materiel and to provide defense on the battlefield. Each chariot was manned by a fixed number of warriors, and the number of war chariots owned by a state was a mark of its strength. A strong state was known as a "state of a thousand chariots" or even "state of ten thousand chariots," according to the number of chariots it possessed.

42. Three jade figurines. Height 1 1/4″ to 1 1/2″. They have a primitive, unsophisticated simplicity. The hair styles are probably those of the White Di people

had such ritual vessels as *ding* and *dou*, which suggests that the White Di state had recognized the authority of the king of Zhou and regarded itself as his vassal. With the passage of time, the White Di and Huaxia finally became identical in their mode of life, thinking, economy, and culture.

During the twenty years of Wei occupation, Zhongshan was governed by Li Ke, an able Wei minister. He took measures to spread the Huaxia culture in Zhongshan, especially in the manufacture of iron tools to develop production, the establishing of public order, and the equal treatment of White Di and Huaxia peoples. As a result, conditions in Zhongshan changed greatly and the merging of the two peoples was hastened.

The Wei influence gradually diminished with the reestablishment of Zhongshan, but throughout the reigns of Duke Huan, Duke Cheng, and King Cuo the policies of Li Ke were followed, with slight modifications. The Zhongshan rulers regarded themselves as vassals of the king of Zhou and adopted the Huaxia system of governmental organization and ritual. No longer a nomadic people, the White Di made much progress in agriculture, industry, and crafts. Iron *jue* (pickax), *ben* (adze), *lian* (sickle), *chan* (shovel), and *chu* (hoe) were implements widely used, and there were workshops for pottery and articles of bone and iron. As clothing, the White Di now wore the loose garments of the Huaxia instead of their national tight-fitting dress. In battle they adopted the Huaxia war chariot, seldom resorting to their own martial art of shooting from horseback.

Traces of the White Di culture are still present in the relics unearthed from the Zhongshan tombs. The three-pronged bronze standard top for ritual use, fifty-six inches high, was a symbol of the royal authority of Zhongshan. Tent supports and household utensils, though few in number, were apparently those used in their nomadic life. And the horn-shaped topknots seen in the jade figurines of women probably reflect a hair style of the White Di women.

As the differences vanish between White Di and Huaxia artifacts, one sees the natural outcome of their interchange and mutual influence, which enabled them to merge into the political entity of Zhongshan.

The Fall of Zhongshan

Repeated subjugation and national rehabilitation left its mark on Zhongshan's history, which lasted more than 300 years; in comparison with Fi and Gu, the other two small states founded by the same race, Zhongshan survived much the longest. Its zenith of glory came during the rules of Duke Huan, Duke Cheng, and King Cuo; its decline began after Jie Zhi ascended the throne.

In the meantime King Lin Wu of Zhao, actively preparing for war against Zhongshan in the north, exhorted his people to take on the tight-sleeved tunic of the northern nomadic tribes and learn their art of fighting from horseback with bows and arrows instead of from the conventional war chariot.[2]

In 305 B.C. King Lin Wu led an expedition against Zhongshan and extended his territory to within fifty miles of Lingshuo, capital of Zhongshan. Four years later he waged another war and Zhongshan, too weak to resist, lost another large area to Zhao. Jie Zhi fled to the State of Qi, where he died two years later. After his death his son, Shang, was crowned king of Zhongshan, but with only a narrow tract of territory remaining, Zhongshan had not long to survive. It was conquered for the last time by Qi and Yan in 296 B.C., and King Shang was sent back to his ancestral homeland, Yushi (present-day Yanan in Shaanxi).

[2] War chariots first appeared during the Shang Dynasty. They came into wider use during the Spring and Autumn Period. Because the chariots were found to be less maneuverable than the cavalry of the northern tribes, King Lin Wu of Zhao formed a cavalry unit along those lines during the Warring States Period—the first cavalry unit formed by the Huaxia people. Subsequently the war chariot fell into oblivion.

43. Dragon-shaped pendant of yellow jade. Length 9 1/4", width 4 1/2", thickness 1/8"

44. (*overleaf, above left*) Bronze plate inlaid with gold and silver, incised with a groundplan of the underground palace of the king of Zhongshan; a 450-character inscription describes in detail the location and sizes of the structures in the palace. It is the earliest architectural plan found in China. Length 37 1/2", width 19", thickness 3/8"

45. (*overleaf, below left*) Jade toads. The toad, together with the turtle and the crane, were symbols of good luck in ancient China

46. (*overleaf, right*) Three-pronged bronze standard top for ritual use, signifying the royal authority of Zhongshan. Height 56", width 31 1/2"

47. Square *hu*, bronze ritual vessel. Height 24 1/4″. An inscription of more than 400 characters describes Zhongshan's participation in a war waged by the State of Qi against Yan

48. Three-legged round bronze cauldron, a ritual vessel. Height 20″. Bears an inscription of some 400 characters similar in content to that on the square *hu* (Plate 47)

49. Winged mythical creature, bronze with gold and silver inlay. Length 15″, height 10″. An imaginative work, it combines a dragon's head and a tiger-like body with wings of a phoenix to symbolize dignity, strength, and good luck

50. Bronze base inlaid with gold and silver in the shape of a tiger with a deer locked in its teeth. Length 19 1/2″, height 8 1/2″. The hind legs are larger in proportion to those of a real tiger, making the beast appear even more powerful. Its curled tail adds much to its charm, and its head looks like that of a Chinese folk toy tiger

The Gold- and Silver-Inlaid Bronzes of Zhongshan

Of the thirty Zhongshan tombs excavated at the site of Ling-shuo, two are royal tombs that belonged to King Cuo and another ruler. Over 19,000 artifacts were discovered in these tombs and in the funeral pits around them. The most valuable are the bronzes, particularly bronzes with gold and silver inlays.

Inlaying with gold or silver is the ornamenting of the bronze surface by cutting grooves and setting in threads or segments of gold, silver, or other materials. The technique became highly refined as well as popular in the fabrication of bronze objects in this period.

The tiger devouring a deer, which is actually a bronze base inlaid with gold and silver, is the product of realism combined with imagination. Likewise is the winged mythical creature with silver inlay. The extraordinary gold and silver patterns on the twisting surfaces are beautifully shaped and seem to be bursting with vitality.

39

51. (*below*) Rectangular tray resting on a bronze stand inlaid with gold and silver dragon, phoenix, and deer motifs. Height 14″. The riches of Zhongshan and its luxury-loving rulers provided their artisans with ample opportunity to use their talents. Great works of art are the product not only of the painstaking labor of their talented creators but also of the patrons' love of luxury

52. (*opposite*) Bronze lamp with fifteen oil cups. Height 31 3/4″. Made in eight detachable parts, easy to dismantle for filling and cleaning; the lamp is of wonderful workmanship

One of the wonders among the excavated bronzes is the rectangular tray that rests on its stand made of dragon, phoenix, and deer motifs. The four supports are composed of the intertwined bodies of four dragons and four phoenixes, and at the corners of the whole are four deer, their heads raised as if they were just waking up with a start. Though complicated in its structure, this work is executed in perfect proportions, every part in its ideal place. The motifs are joined by riveting and welding. Surely this tray table is one of the best testaments to the highly developed culture of Zhongshan.

The bronze lamp with fifteen oil cups is another prized piece, showing the fine workmanship and superb casting technique of the Zhongshan culture. The lamp takes the form of a tree with the oil cups as its fruit. Birds and monkeys are singing and frolicking along its branches. Under the tree two men raise their arms toward the monkeys above, hoping that the animals might playfully drop their fruit. Imbued with touches of everyday activity, this work of art tells much about the rich imagination of its creator.

Other gold- and silver-inlaid bronze objects, jade carvings, and black pottery with veiled decorations are finds of the highest artistic value.

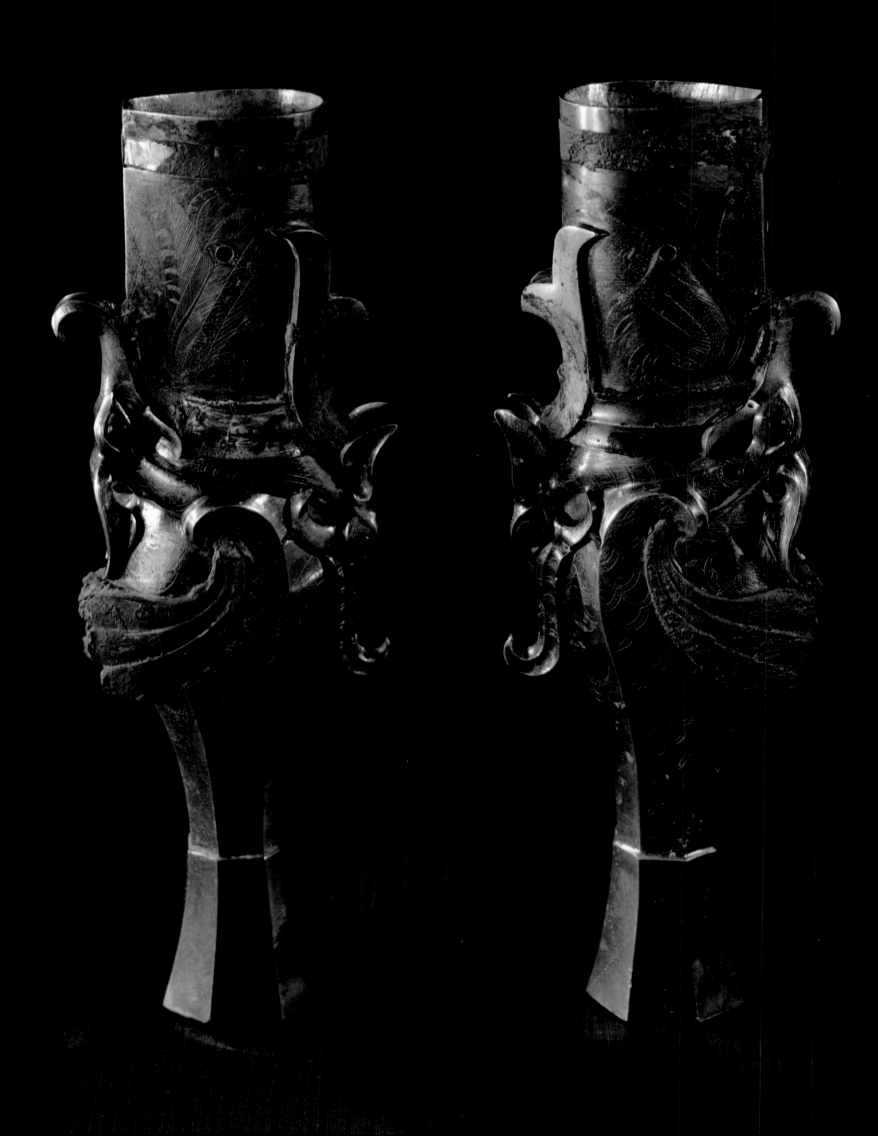

53. (*opposite*) Decorative gilt bronze butt-ends, for weapons carried by guard of honor

54. Black pottery wine vessel, with head and tail in lapwing shape. Well polished, with veiled patterns. Height 11 1/4″, width 13 1/2″. A large number of black pottery vessels were found in the Zhongshan tombs at Pingshan

55. A green liquid and the circular bronze vessel that contained it when found in the tomb of King Cuo

56. A dark green liquid and the spherical bronze vessel that contained it when found in King Cuo's tomb. The vessel held about six pints of liquor and was half full

Ancient Liquids

The two liquids, by far the oldest known in China, were found in the tomb of King Cuo. Obviously, they were funerary offerings. More than a dozen vessels for wine, all made of bronze, were discovered in the tomb. Two of these actually contained wine, one only half filled. The other wine vessels were probably full when they were buried, but their contents evaporated because they were not tightly sealed.

The liquids and the wine vessels in the tomb may indicate that during his lifetime the tomb occupant was fond of drinking. Drinking seems to have been popular among the Zhongshan people. The scanty information in ancient historical records tells us that Zhongshan people, men and women alike, were fond of sensuous pleasures, such as drinking, making merry, and singing sad melodies. In addition, the inhabitants of the land where Zhongshan was located had been known, under the Shang Dynasty, to indulge in drinking.

When opened, the two vessels containing the liquids emitted an ambrosial aroma. A chemical analysis revealed the presence of alcohol, sugar, fat, and a dozen other ingredients—perhaps a kind of hot buttered rum! How had it remained in liquid state for so long a time? What changes had taken place in it? These interesting questions still await a scientific explanation.

43

3. Music, Craftsmanship, and Tragedy in the Tomb of Marquis Yi

Pre-Qin Musical Instruments

The county of Sui Xian in Hubei Province has a long history, like many of the counties in South China. During the Eastern Zhou Period (770 B.C.–221 B.C.) it was known from historical data as the State of Sui. The Queshui and the Yunshui rivers meet outside the county seat and empty into the Changjiang.

The county suddenly achieved fame in 1978, when an ancient tomb was discovered at Leigudun. Inscriptions on the bronzes found in it identify the occupant as Marquis Yi of the State of Zeng. A bronze *fu*-bell given to him by Prince Hui Wang of Chu in the 56th year of his reign (433 B.C.) indicates that the tomb is of that year or somewhat later. Therefore it can be maintained that the tomb belongs early in the Warring States Period (475 B.C.–221 B.C.), some 2,400 years ago.

The 7,000 burial objects included bronze articles, musical instruments, weapons, horse and chariot ornaments, articles of gold and jade, lacquerware, articles of wood and bamboo, and bamboo strips. The large number of musical instruments is fascinating, and the bronzes are exquisite.

The panpipes, *jian*-drum, ten-string zither, and five-string zither are the first of their kind to be discovered in China; ten-string and five-string zithers are mentioned nowhere in historical documents concerning China's musical instruments. The stone-

All works illustrated in this chapter are in the Hubei Provincial Museum, Wuhan

57. (*opposite*) Bronze figure. Overall height 46″, weight 706 lbs. One of six figures used to support the beams at ends and angle

58. Gold bowl with lid. Height 4 1/4″, diameter at mouth 6″; weight 4 3/4 lbs. The largest gold object of its kind from the pre-Qin period. The openwork gold ladle was found inside the bowl

59. Gold cup. Overall height 4 1/2″, diameter of the mouth 3″

61

62

63

60. Designs of inner coffin (detail)

61. The inner coffin of Marquis Yi.
Length 8', width 4', height 4' 1/4". It
is made of thick wooden planks
painted red, with decorative patterns
in gold, yellow, and black

62. During the excavation

63. The pit of the tomb of Marquis Yi
of Zeng, seen from the air. 69' east–
west, 53' north–south

64. The four tomb chambers: north, east,
central, and west. The remains of
Marquis Yi lay in the east (right)
chamber

65. (*opposite*) *Fu*-bell. Entire height
36 1/2"; weight 236 lbs. The 31-character
inscription states that it was given to
Marquis Yi in the 56th year of the
reign of Hui Wang, Prince of Chu

64

66. Lacquer box in shape of a mandarin duck. Height 6 1/2″, length 8″. The lid is on the back of the duck, and the head is movable

67. Lacquer food container on wooden base, with lid. Height 9 3/4″. Elaborate square ears at each side. Bowl, ears, stem, and foot were carved separately

68. Lacquer teapoy (reconstruction). Length 23 3/4″, width 8 1/2″, height 20 1/4″

69. Lacquer table (reconstruction). Length 54 1/2″, width 21″, height 17 1/2″

70. Lacquer trunk decorated with twenty-eight constellations. Length 32 1/2″, height 17 1/2″. A green dragon is represented on one end of the lid, a white tiger on the other. At the center is the Big Dipper surrounded by the names of the constellations. Earliest record in China of the astronomical constellations

71. (opposite) Lacquer stag resting. Height 34″, length 19 1/2″

72. *Jian*-drum (reconstruction). Length 40″, diameter 31 1/2″. The frame of the drum is wood, the face is hide. A wooden shaft that goes through the body is fixed into the center of the bronze stand

73. Bronze stand of the *jian*-drum. Height 20″, width 31 1/2″. Sixteen large dragons interwine with one another to form rhythmic patterns. Smaller dragons cling to the large ones' heads, bodies, and tails. The inlays are turquoises. This is the first object of its kind ever found

chimes and bells were still in their original position when discovered, an altogether extraordinary circumstance. The bamboo flute, which is played horizontally, is the oldest of its kind yet found. The panpipes are similar in form to those in ancient murals and stone carvings, as well as to those used in Eastern Europe today. In pre-Qin times they were known as "*lai*," which might bear some relation to their Romanian name, "*nai*."

The sixty-four bronze *bian*-bells together with the *fu*-bell presented by the Prince of Chu are arranged in eight groups according to size and pitch, and hang in three rows on the L-shaped frame. The wooden beams of the frame are supported by six bronze atlas-like figures and have decorative bronze finials. The whole structure is solid and enduring, and has stood intact for 2,400 years.

The *bian*-bells are true to the inscriptions that specify the notes for each of them. The scale of the whole set is not unlike the diatonic in C major, and the range is five octaves. The bells can play music ancient or modern, foreign or Chinese. The middle row is melodious and resonant, and on it can be played the melody. The bottom row is deep and sonorous, as for an accompaniment.

The predecessor of the *bian*-bell is the *nao*-bell of the Shang Dynasty (c. 16th century B.C.–11th century B.C.). Constructed with the mouth of the bell upward, the *nao* is arranged in groups of three for playing simple tunes. This upward bell developed into the hanging bell during the Western Zhou (11th century

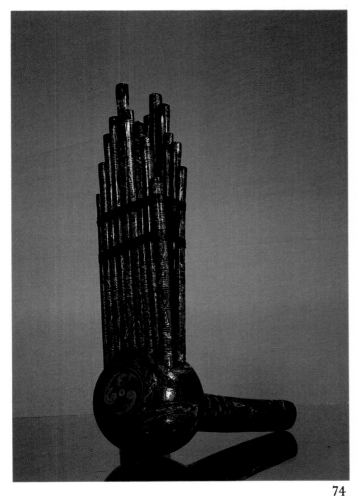

74

76

75

77

78

79

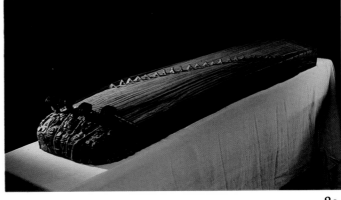

80

74. *Sheng*-pipe (reconstruction). The body is 8″ long. Eighteen pipes of bamboo with a vibrating reed inside each pipe

75. The 10-string zither (reconstruction). Length 26 1/2″

76. Panpipes (reconstruction). Length 8 3/4″, overall width 5 1/4″. It is made of 13 fine bamboo pipes. The tomb contained two panpipes

77. 5-string instrument (reconstruction). Length 45 1/2″. Carved from one piece of wood, it has a soundbox with five holes

78. Two bamboo flutes (reconstructions). Length about 11″. They have seven holes and are played horizontally. The earliest known Chinese specimens

79, 80. The *se*-zither (reconstruction). Length 66 1/2″, width 16 1/2″

81, 82. (*this page and opposite*) The *bian*-bells being excavated. They were in the southwestern part of the central room, most of them hanging in their original places. Beside the bell frame were six wooden hammers and two logs for performance

83, 84. Stone-chimes (frame is original, chimes are reconstructions). The thirty-two chimes are made of jade and stone. The inscription on each of them explains the pitch. The frame is of bronze, length 84″, height 43″. Fantastic animals support the stone-chimes frame

B.C.–771 B.C.). Marquis Yi's *bian*-bells have developed into a form designed for playing more complicated melodies.

The stone-chimes, thirty-two pieces of jade and stone, are divided into four groups. Few of the pieces have survived intact, but remnants of the inscriptions explain the tuning system for the stone-chimes and the *bian*-bells. The stone-chimes sound clear

85. The *bian*-bells. There are 64 *bian*-bells, and the *fu*-bell presented by the Prince of Chu. The largest bell is 60″ high and weighs 447 lbs., the smallest is 8″ high and 5 1/4 lbs. The total weight is 2 3/4 tons. All the bells are inscribed. The L-shaped frame is made of bronze and wooden beams. Entire length 25′, height 9′; composed of 245 movable parts

and strong, and must have been quite a spectacle when they were played together with the bells.

These musical instruments show the developments made during the Spring and Autumn and the Warring States periods, and thus they are firsthand material for the study of history before the Qin Period. Pre-Qin music is lost to us; although we know how the chimes and bells were played, we must imagine the sound of the music.

The Height of Craftsmanship

The 140 bronzes include decorative articles, articles for ritual and for daily use. Many are works of art in low relief, and high relief, decorated with inlays or fretwork.

The bronzes are large in size and were found in great numbers. They demonstrate clearly the amazing technical level of bronze-casting in the early Warring States Period.

86. Bronze stork with antlers of a stag.
Height 56″; weight 84 1/4 lbs.

56

The sixty-five bells weigh almost three tons in all. The full height of the largest one is five feet, and it weighs 450 pounds. One of the bronze supporting figures weighs 650 pounds. The bronze frame of the outer coffin of Marquis Yi weighs 3 1/2 tons. Its beams are I-shaped, U-shaped, and L-shaped, similar to modern steel counterparts. This bronze structure is the first of its kind to be found, and the bronze is still in good condition. Initial calculations put the total weight of this bronze frame at 11 tons, an unprecedented number. Technically, 12 tons of copper, tin, and lead were required as raw material. We have mentioned in Chapter 1 that a 1-ton bronze cauldron was found in the Yin Ruins; the discovery of this 11-ton frame in the tomb of the marquis of a small state shows that bronze-casting technique in the Warring States Period had developed greatly since the Yin and Shang dynasties.

During the Warring States Period the transition was made from the Bronze Age to the Iron Age. Iron-casting developed after bronze-casting. The casting of a sizable bronze calls for a large furnace, high furnace temperatures, and a strong bellows, all factors necessary for smelting and casting iron.

The shape of the articles and their decoration and technology also represent new achievements in technique. We should look, for instance, at the *bian*-bells, so popular during the Warring States Period. All previous bells are cast in single molds to assure good tonal quality. But the molds of these *bian*-bells consist of dozens of sections, and the decorative patterns were put on later still. The superb workmanship creates a sense of three dimensions, yet careful checking finds no fault in technology, and the bells are in correct pitch. This is no easy achievement even with modern technology.

The set of wine vessel and tray is the most exquisite of all the bronzes we know. It also reflects a major change in the casting process, for the openwork decoration was probably made with the "lost-wax" method. The decoration on both pieces consists of two parts, the openwork and its supports. The openwork is made in separate sections while the supports are mostly connected with each other. The decoration combines intricate roughness with varied smoothness in a beautifully wrought design that is magnificent and impressive.

The bronze decoration bears no trace of forging or soldering. The complexity of the forms makes impossible the use of a single mold or even sectional molds, and the lost-wax process must have been followed. Judging from the intricate curves of the supports, the wax used was soft, perhaps a mixture of beeswax, rosin, and fat.

This remarkably fine workmanship makes it clear that the lost-wax method of casting was already thoroughly understood,

87. Bronze vessel for cooling or warming wine. Entire height 24 1/4", mouth 29" square, weight 371 lbs. Inside is a square bronze pot to hold the wine

88, 89. Bronze wine vessel and tray. Height of vessel 13"; weight 17 1/2 lbs. Height of plate 9 1/2", diameter 18 5/8"; weight 42 lbs. When found, the vessel was on the tray. The decoration is a fine openwork, probably cast by the lost-wax process

and that the use of the method must have begun much earlier. The traditional theory, that the lost-wax method came to China from India together with Buddhism, is no longer valid, for the date of this tomb (after 433 B.C.) precedes the spread of Buddhism (after 206 B.C.). Thus the discovery of these fretwork decorations has great significance for students of the history of science as well as of art and archeology.

Tian Gong Kai Wu, the famous scientific work of ancient China, records the technique of lost-wax casting, directions for making the wax, and the ratio of the weight of bronze to that of wax. Many lost-wax castings of the Ming and Qing dynasties have survived: the bronze lions, elephants, mythical animals, and

90. Twin bronze wine
    vessels. Height
    43 3/4″, diameter of
    mouth 12 3/4″

oxen in Beijing's former Imperial Palace and Summer Palace are only a few of many fine examples.

The States of Zeng, Sui, and Chu, and the Slaves' Tragic Fate

The Zhou overthrew the Shang Dynasty in the 11th century B.C. The Shang capital fell into ruins, known to us today as the Yin Ruins (see Chapter 1). Zhou established its capital at Hao near present-day Xi'an in Shaanxi Province. The ruler of Zhou proclaimed himself the Son of Heaven. He granted titles and territories to his own clan and to meritorious officials, thereby establishing many suzerain states. China entered into a stage of stability that lasted for two and a half centuries, the period known as the Western Zhou (1027 B.C.–771 B.C.).

In 771 B.C. Hao was seized by the Rong tribe, and the State of Zhou moved its capital east to Luoyang (in Henan Province). After 770 B.C. the state was known as the Eastern Zhou, but it began its decline. The petty states were no longer obedient and paid no tribute to Zhou, but they fought among themselves for power. Thus started a period of turbulence; China entered the Warring States Period in 475 B.C. Numerous wars broke out; the strong conquered the weak, and the large the small; alliances were frequently formed and as frequently broken.

During the Eastern Zhou, a number of states were formed within Hubei Province. Chu was the strongest, and Sui came next; later, Chu annexed all the other states. Nowhere is there mention of a State of Zeng within the territory, yet the tomb of Marquis Yi, Prince of Zeng, has been unearthed, and bronze articles from the State of Zeng have been found in the surrounding counties—Jingshan, Zaoyang, and Xinye. Evidently there was a State of Zeng. A number of questions have thus been raised. What is the relation between the archeologists' Zeng and the historians' Sui? Are they different names for the same state, or are they two independent states? How could they have coexisted in such a narrow area?

The *fu*-bell in Marquis Yi's tomb, given by the Prince of Chu, occupies the most prominent place on the frame among the *bian*-bells. This indicates the respect accorded to Chu by Zeng, and the good relations they maintained. But what else passed between them?

Marquis Yi died at about age 45. Inside his tomb were found twenty-one smaller coffins, the occupants all girls between 15 and 25 years old. Eight of the coffins were placed in the same chamber with the marquis's coffin, the other thirteen in another room. The outside of the coffins are painted with colorful designs, and some funerary objects are inside. The skeletons were intact, with no sign of wounds. The twenty-one girls who were buried with their master were in their prime years; probably they first committed suicide or were somehow deceived into death. The *bian*-bells, stone-chimes, and other musical instruments indicate that Marquis Yi liked music, and these girls must be concubines, singers, and dancers. We can imagine them dancing to melodious music while the master entertains his guests at a feast. When he dies, their young lives too are ended by tragic means.

This custom is more "civilized" than that seen before, in the Shang slave pits of the Yin Ruins. It was a custom during the Yin-Shang period to kill at the burial ceremony a great number of slaves owned by the deceased. Later, in the Qin and Han periods, pottery or wooden figures were used instead of human beings. But the old custom had persisted, for Marquis Yi, who lived 600 years after the Yin-Shang, still included human beings among his funerary articles.

In the next chapter we discuss the lifesize pottery warriors from the tomb of the First Emperor of Qin. He was a cruel and ambitious ruler, but he did not dare to kill 6,000 soldiers or bury them with him. Hence the burial of the pottery warriors in battle array; nevertheless, history records that he caused a number of young girls to be buried alive with him after his death.

4. Qin Dynasty Warriors and Horses: A Great Terracotta Army of 220 B.C.

Mount Lishan, the Mausoleum of the First Emperor of Qin, and the Discovery of the Terracotta Warriors and Horses

Mount Lishan is some fifteen miles east of the famous Chinese ancient capital Xi'an (originally Changan), now the capital of Shaanxi Province. The mountain is densely wooded and looks like a recumbent horse, which explains its name, for *Li* means a dark blue horse; the name might also have come from the ancient state of Li Yong, which built its capital there.

Mount Lishan has long been associated in Chinese history with well-known legends having a romantic flavor. In the eighth century B.C., for example, toward the close of Western Zhou, Emperor You suddenly ordered a beacon fire to be lighted on top of Mount Lishan. Princes and dukes came riding to the rescue with their armies, only to find he had played a practical joke on them. At the sight Be Si, the emperor's favorite concubine, who was said never to have smiled, burst out laughing, but at a joke that spelled the doom of Western Zhou. For when Quan Yong, a neighboring state, later launched an attack and the emperor had beacon fires lighted again, the dukes and princes thought it another hoax and refused to come. Thus Western Zhou fell. The episode has become known in history as "A smile of beauty overturned an empire," and "Playing a joke on the princes with beacon fire."

And another poignant legend: there is a hot springs on Lishan. Here, in the eighth century A.D., Li Longchi, who was Emperor Xuan Zhong of the Tang Dynasty, played and feasted with his imperial concubine, a peerless beauty named Yang Yuhuan. A glimpse of their court life is provided by Po Chuyi (772–846), the Tang poet: ". . . It was early spring. They bathed her in the Flower-Pure Pool which warmed and smoothed the creamy-tinted crystal of her skin." The emperor and his concubine had pledged to be "man and wife to the end of time" in the Palace of Eternal Life on Lishan. But General An Lushan

All works illustrated in this chapter are in the Museum of Qin Dynasty Terracotta Warriors and Horses, Xi'an

91. (*opposite*) Restoring pottery figure

65

92. The Mausoleum of the First Emperor
of Qin

staged an armed rebellion, and the emperor and his concubine were forced to flee the capital. On the way the emperor's troops rebelled; to save his skin the emperor, in great distress, allowed them to strangle the peerless beauty in his presence. ". . . The men of the army stopped, not one of them would stir until under their horses' hoofs they might trample those moth-eyebrows." The plot of *The Palace of Eternal Life*, a famous drama of the early Qing Dynasty, is based on this tragic romance.

We now leave the Tang Dynasty and go back more than a thousand years, to the First Emperor of Qin (259 B.C.–210 B.C.) and to his tomb.

The tomb stands on the northern bank of the Wei River, with Mount Lishan to the southeast. Soon after the young King Zheng succeeded to the throne in 246 B.C., at the age of 13, he ordered the building of his mausoleum to begin. The large-scale construction of the mausoleum for the First Emperor of Qin, as he came to be known, was undertaken in 221 B.C., after he had unified China and proclaimed himself First Emperor.

The mausoleum is actually a lavish underground palace on a gigantic scale. According to historical records, over 700,000 "criminals" were conscripted to build it; it was some 140 feet high with a 5-*li*, or 3-mile, circumference. Dug deep into the ground, it was reinforced with molten bronze against subterranean streams. The tomb contained whole courts, with places reserved for officials, and a great horde of treasure. Quicksilver was pooled to create seas and waterways, and mechanisms made them flow. Candles of whale fat illuminated the burial chamber. At strategic points were placed crossbows, mechanically triggered to shoot at any intruder. When the emperor's body was moved

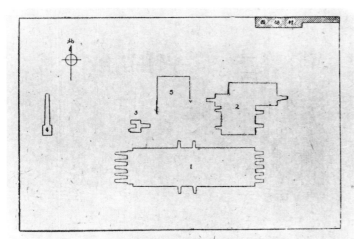

93. Pits Nos. 1, 2, and 3

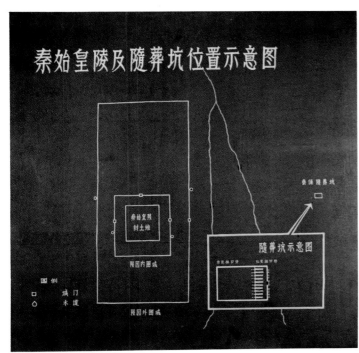

94. Sketch map with locations of the
    mausoleum and pits

95. Partly restored masonry and wooden
    framework of Pit No. 1

into the burial chamber, all of his concubines who had not borne sons were herded in too, and in death they kept their emperor company.

Today a mound of tamped earth 130 feet high still stands above the mausoleum on a base about 1,600 feet square. The mound is landscaped on four sides like a pyramid. It is surrounded by a square inner wall a mile and a half around with gates on the east, west, and north, and an oblong outer wall four miles around with a gate on the east. The existing gates aboveground were built later.

In March 1974, peasants sinking a well a mile east of the mausoleum dug up lifesize terracotta figures. Archeologists came to investigate, prospect, study, and excavate. Finally access to the vast mausoleum was permitted, to reveal a powerful Qin army buried in formation 2,200 years ago.

The First Emperor of Qin

96. Site of Pit No. 1, May 1975. In the background, Mount Lishan

In 221 B.C. Ying Zheng, the First Emperor of Qin, unified China and thereby became a noted historical figure.

The period 475 B.C.–221 B.C. is known to history as the Warring States Period, during which the central area of China was dominated by seven states—Qi, Chi, Yan, Zhao, Han, Wei, and Qin. Private interests of the rulers led to frequent strife among them. These states possessed rich human and material resources, a population altogether of twenty million. In a major campaign hundreds of thousands of troops might be thrown into battle by both sides. The pattern of warfare developed from chariot formation to field operations with encirclement by infantry and cavalry. Wars sometimes continued in a stalemate for years.

When King Ying Zheng was crowned Emperor of Qin his territory extended from today's Shaanxi, Gansu, Ningxia, and Sichuan to Shanxi, Henan, Hubei, and Guizhou, and its population was the largest of all the states. Starting in 230 B.C., Qin befriended the faraway states and attacked the nearer ones, thereby splitting up the other six states. In ten years he had accomplished China's unification, putting an end in 221 B.C. to the separatist rule which the princes had practiced since the Western Zhou (11th century B.C.–771 B.C.), and establishing a feudal empire with authority centered in himself. Combining *huang* and *di*, the words for sage kings of the legendary past, with the word *shi*, meaning first, Ying Zheng proclaimed himself Qin Shihuangdi, the First Emperor of Qin. His successors were to be titled Second Emperor, Third Emperor, and so on.

A talented statesman with great ambitions, the emperor divided his domain into thirty-six prefectures, each made up of

97. The Museum of Qin Dynasty Terracotta Warriors and Horses, opened October 1, 1979

counties. He established a set of political systems under a centralized authority, and made decisions on all important state affairs, appointed or removed central and local officials, standardized the currency, weights and measures, and written language, and promulgated a uniform code of laws. He ordered border cities of the warring states to dismantle their defenses, and highways to be constructed to strengthen land communication throughout the country. He dispatched troops to attack the Huns in the north, to pacify the southern Yue, and to garrison the Five Ranges. And by his order the Great Wall was built, to defend the northern boundaries of Qin, Yan, and Zhao.

But the First Emperor also enforced severe laws, imposed heavy taxes and levies, and requisitioned numerous services from his people: some 500,000 persons drafted to garrison the Five Ranges; 300,000 more stationed to guard against the Huns; 500,-000 were sent to build the Great Wall; and 1,500,000 were conscripted to construct palaces and tombs. With various other forms

of services added, the grand total topped 3,000,000, or 15 percent of the total of 20 million. The suffering of the people can well be imagined. "Long has the world been afflicted by the rule of Qin!" Peasant revolts broke out soon after the emperor's death in 210 B.C. Three years later, Qin was overthrown.

A Qin Military Formation Reappears

Three vaults containing a great number of terracotta warriors and horses have been found. Pit No. 1 was discovered in March 1974. Probing by archeologists, then tentative digs, established the presence of an underground structure of wood and masonry 688 feet from east to west and 200 feet from north to south, an area of almost 4 acres. The roof had burned and collapsed, crushing most of the figures; only a small number remained intact, but the broken pieces lay strewn where they had been crushed and the figures could be restored. In all there were

98, 99. (*this page and overleaf*) Pit No. 1, eastern end. Part of the formation of pottery figures has been restored according to the original positions

72

100. Restoring a pottery figure

101. Reassembling a pottery figure

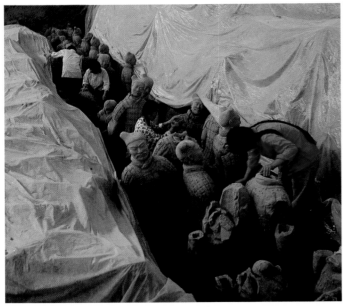

102. Archeologists and young helpers digging and sorting at the site

103. The forms of wheel and frame of an ancient battle chariot are plainly visible

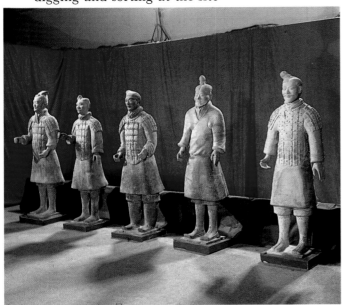

104. Pottery warriors restored

105. A corner of Pit No. 1

6,000 pottery soldiers; six 4-horse chariots were lined up in 11 rows that were composed principally of infantrymen. The vault floor was paved with bricks.

Two years later, in May 1976, some 68 feet northeast of Pit No. 1, an L-shaped vault was discovered having an area of 2 1/2 acres. Pit No. 2 contains over 1,400 clay figures of horses and men in a formation principally of horses, chariots, and cavalry, supported by infantry, armed and unarmed. Pit No. 3, found at almost the same time, is northwest of Pit No. 1; the smallest of the three, it is 5,600 feet square, and it contains 73 warriors all holding short-range weapons, arranged in positions guarding the commanders who ride in a chariot. After trial digs, Pits No. 2 and No. 3 have been refilled with earth to await further excavation and sorting.

106. Archer ready to release the crossbow

Over Pit No. 1 has been built an on-site museum, the Museum of Qin Dynasty Terracotta Warriors and Horses. Visitors who look down over railings at the lifesize clay warriors and horses arranged 2,200 years ago on the vault floor 20 feet below the ground will sense the power of the First Emperor of Qin who, as noted in historical records, "led a million armored soldiers, a thousand chariots, and ten thousand horses, to conquer and to gloat over the world." Two hundred and ten terracotta warriors, facing south, line up three deep in a gallery that is 200 feet from north to south at the eastern end of the pit. They form the vanguard, and except for their three armored officers, all wear knee-length tunics and thin-soled, tightly laced shoes with black cloth leggings; they held weapons, either bows or cross-bows. From their dress and weapons they may have been "assault troops," ready to charge the enemy. Facing east behind them in eleven corridors are thirty-eight rows of foot soldiers and chariots. The outer corridors on either side and at the western end accommodate other files of warriors; facing north, south, and west, respectively, and holding their weapons, they seem to be guards of the main army, ready to repulse any attack from the flank or rear. The disposition is a well-ordered, tightly knit battle formation.

Excavation and Restoration

The pottery figures occupy a vast area. The museum is open to visitors, but the work of excavation and repair continues. Tourists can see restored figures in one part of the museum as well as the original destruction, while the work of excavation and repair goes on elsewhere in the museum.

Workers have carefully dug up broken clay pieces (bulldozers and mechanical excavators are out of question here), cleaned them gently with brushes, made notes and drawings of each, and photographed them. The restorers then do their work, determining carefully the thickness of each piece, and its shape, color, and location. Finally hundreds of pieces are glued together to form one intact clay warrior or horse. Looking for a missing piece can take hours or even days. Hard work has brought about the reappearance of the terracotta army.

History and Art

"A million strong with a thousand chariots."

"Engage an enemy and be sure to vanquish it, storm a city and take it without fail, make a clean sweep of all that dare to stand in the way, and put several thousand *li* of land under the empire's domain . . ."

So historians described the armed power of Qin and commended the First Emperor for unifying China. The terracotta warriors and horses re-create this martial image.

107, 108, 109. Distinctive hair styles of warriors

110, 111. Square-toed sandals and shoes

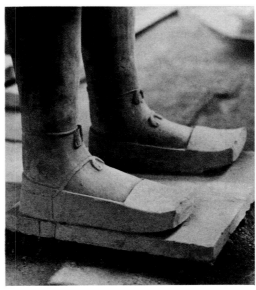

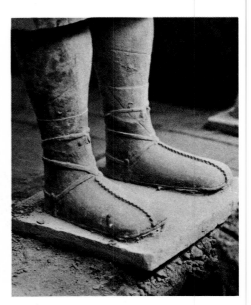

The clay figures show the different accouterments, features, status, and mien of foot soldiers, officers, and cavalrymen, and of their horses. Soldiers range in height from 68 to 74 inches, and are of two types. The first type wears a high-collared garment under a knee-length tunic, with belt tied in the middle, and the hair in a chignon tied a little to the right; sandals are square toed, with leggings above. The position of the arms and the weapons at hand suggest that this type may have held bows, crossbows, or spears, or carried sabers in their belts. The second type wears a knee-length tunic beneath his armored jacket, and square-toed sandals with leggings. All foot soldiers wear their hair in topknots, or soft-brim caps. Chariot warriors too wear leggings and caps, or tie back their hair in chignons. Some armored soldiers held bows, crossbows, or spears, and some carried bronze swords in their belts.

Cavalrymen are clad in short armored battle vests and boots with leggings. They hold the reins in their right hands and bows

112. Cavalryman and horse. Beautifully modeled, the horse has an elegant bridle and halter beaded with small pieces of stones. The cavalryman wears a soft-brimmed cap fastened under the chin with leather thongs
113. Charioteer in position behind chariot. To engage the enemy, he mounts the vehicle
114. Charioteer poised with reins
115. Kneeling archer ready to shoot
116. Commander, who looks older, more sedate and dignified than his men. He wears armor made of small plates, and a cap with double tails

112

113

114

115

116

117. Horses, four to a chariot,
wait to be restored

118, 119, Many of the pottery figures are
120. individualized, the features and
formation of their faces reflecting real
appearance

in their left. The horses are of sturdy build, their heads raised, ears pricked up, and eyes open wide. Bridles are made of leather and have a solid feel.

The kneeling archers have an animated pose, with right knee on the ground and left leg bent, the body inclined slightly forward and a little toward the left, eyes looking sharply left. Hands are poised to cradle the bow, ready to shoot.

The stalwart commander towers six-and-a-half feet tall. His cap has double folds, and he is dressed in a battle tunic covered with an armored apron of small, elaborate plates; he has knotted decorations on shoulders, breast, and back. He once carried a long sword, and his calm and resolute expression bespeaks his rank. The pottery figures are true images of personnel of the Qin army; they are valuable as historical data and exquisite as objects of art.

Early bronze articles of the Shang and Zhou periods bore images such as "slave in tiger's mouth" and "*Taotie* the man-eater" that reflected the superstitious slave society—images perhaps used by the slave owners to terrorize their subjects. By the Warring States Period, certain bronze articles bore depictions of subjects from real life, such as hunting, silkworm culture, and battle. But the sculpture of the Qin terracotta figures is wholly based on reality and draws its material from actual life. It reflects the spirit of the times of the First Emperor of Qin as he unified China with his powerful army, and it brings out a national style of lucidity and grandeur. While ancient Greek sculpture excelled in showing the structure and beauty of the human body at rest and in motion, the Qin pottery figures stress the delineation of facial expression to reveal variations of inner character. Through such details as the tilted corner of a mouth, the crow's feet at the eyes, the varied mustaches and hair styles, the statues are endlessly individualized. Some stand erect, bold and fierce; others look cheerful, or express high spirits. The quiet, innocent-looking young man is probably a new recruit; the bearded, smiling middle-aged man seems to be confident of victory, and a brave warrior; the heavy-browed fellow with a square chin is ready to charge the enemy and lay down his life; the sword-carrying commander is lost in deep thought, perhaps reflecting the cares of leadership.

The martial air and combat readiness of the troops and the lively image of each fighter bring to mind the vast battlefield with weapons clanking and warriors charging. The silent figures are frozen into an all-conquering heroism. The horses are sturdy, with broad chests and solid legs, braided tails and cropped forelocks. Their raised heads, dilated nostrils, and pricked-up ears show an alertness that matches the daring of the warriors.

The terracotta warriors and horses are the first instances of a style that reappears in the art of later generations. Some outstanding examples—the sixteen stone carvings of the tomb of Ho

121. A long, very sharp sword

Qubing of Western Han in Maoling, Shaanxi Province, of 117 B.C.; the bronze galloping horse of Eastern Han (see Chapter 7); and the six steeds of Emperor Tai Zhong of the Tang Dynasty (636–637 A.D.) in Zhaoling—may be considered to have developed from the art of the Qin pottery figures. The Qin figures, the first examples of monumental Chinese art, also mark a mature phase of representational sculpture. They are comparable to ancient Greek counterparts.

The Making of the Pottery Figures, and Metallurgical Technology

In the course of mankind's development, pottery and metalwork are two continuously growing techniques. Of the two, pottery was made at much the earlier date.

The Qin warriors and horses are made of coarse gray clay, fired at high temperatures. They were not made from molds, but were modeled individually. Heads, arms, and torsos of warriors were fashioned separately, then joined with clay strips. The hollow heads and torsos were supported by solid clay legs. The legs were apparently made first, then the torso was built up with coils of clay. The cross section of broken figures shows that head and body were made roughcast, then coated with a slip of finer clay on which were carved mouth, nose, eyes, and details of dress. Certain details—ears, beard, armor tacks, and thongs—were modeled separately and attached. The hair was carved elaborately, and shows many distinctive styles of braiding and of forming topknots. Legs, trunk, head, tail, ears, and forelock of the horses were also made separately, and attached while the clay was soft. The hollow trunk was formed of coils of clay strips.

Warriors and horses were originally painted with bright colors. These have faded, from the fire and from being so long underground. What remains on the figures and on the pit floor can give us some idea of the color of the originals. Its basic tones were red, green, and black, set off by blue, purple, white, and yellow; the pottery army had a magnificent harmony of color.

First, the armored warriors: the knee-length tunic of one type was green, with purple-bordered collar and cuffs; the armor was black with white tacks, purple thongs, and yellow buckles, trousers were blue, and black shoes had orange laces. Face, hands,

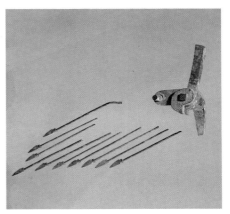

122. The bright colors of the pottery figures have faded or flaked off, from fire and from their long burial. This head still retains traces of mineral pigments which are identifiable as red, green, blue, purple, brown, and yellow

123. Mechanism of crossbow and metal arrowheads

124. Cleaning the molded remains of a quiver with its arrows. Weapons carried by the pottery figures were used in battle

and feet were painted pink; eyes, brows, hair, and beard were black. Another type wore a red knee-length uniform with blue-bordered collar and cuffs, armor was dark brown with red or green tacks and orange thongs, trousers were blue or green, and shoes were black. The horses were black or brown, with white hoofs and teeth. Ears, mouth, and nostrils were red.

Over 10,000 parts of weapons have been unearthed. Bows and crossbows were for long-range combat; spears, swords, broadswords, halberds, and other weapons were for hand-to-hand combat. The bronze swords and arrowheads are as sharp today as when they were cast 2,200 years ago. The weapons too are of fine workmanship, polished, finished, and free of blowholes. Spectrum examination and quantitative analysis tell us that copper and tin alloys are the principal metals, with trace quantities of such metals as nickel, bismuth, zinc, vanadium, silicon, manganese, titanium, molybdenum, cobalt, chromium, and niobium. These metals occurred in the ores of copper, tin, and lead. The sword metal contains 21 percent of tin, refining the texture and increasing hardness. The arrowheads contain less tin but more lead, about 7 percent, making them less hard but more destructive. The varied proportion of the raw materials according to the use of the weapon reflects the progress attained in military science and technology at that time, as well as the knowledge of metals.

Archeological Analysis

The ancient burial system is a mirror of the real ancient world. The mausoleum reflects the kingdom over which the First Emperor of Qin once ruled. He died in July, 210 B.C., and was buried in Mount Lishan in September of that year. So great a number of terracotta warriors and horses could not possibly have been completed in those two or three months; many were certainly fashioned when the emperor was still living. Silt that has accumulated on the pit floor permits the conjecture that the vault burned not long after it was completed, and that it was flooded a number of times. Historical records tell us that Xiang Yu, the king of Chu, entered Shaanxi in 206 B.C., four years after the death of the First Emperor, and set fire to his palaces and dug up his mausoleum. The destruction we see might be the doing of Xiang Yu's army.

What do the terracotta warriors and horses denote or symbolize? Let us examine the arrangement of the pits: Pit No. 1 holds a rectangular formation mainly of infantrymen; north of it is Pit No. 2, which contains phalanxes of cavalrymen and chariots; Pit No. 3, containing many officer figures, is located north of No. 1 and west of No. 2. A fourth pit, about an acre square, lies between Pits No. 2 and No. 3; it is empty, which suggests that work on the terracotta army was abandoned before completion, perhaps due to the peasant revolt led by Chen Xing and Wu Guang, which led to the swift doom of Qin.

Archeologists consider the vaults to be an integral whole. Pit No. 3 appears to be a command unit for the armies in Pits No. 1 and No. 2: first, the warriors there are arrayed as though protecting the commanders instead of in combat formation; second, they hold a kind of bronze weapon known as *yueh*, used for ritual purposes rather than actual combat; third, the chariot in Pit No. 3, unlike those in the other pits, has a painted canopy denoting its owner's rank. Fourth, Pit No. 3 consists of three architectural units: the main hall, the chariot house and stable, and all-purpose rooms, laid out like field headquarters of a garrison commander. This formation could represent the emperor's honor guard, or the Qin army on its eastern expedition to unify China by conquering the six states in Shandong, or the garrison of the capital of Xianyang. The question is still under discussion.

The organizational scheme of the mausoleum, with its tall mound and inner and outer walls, apparently symbolizes an ideal imperial city. The inner part represents the emperor's "forbidden city" in real life, and the outer part stands for the periphery of the imperial city. The palace where the emperor lived, as represented by its underground counterpart, and the city of Xianyang were both guarded by troops. The guards of the capital during the Qin period could be divided into the imperial bodyguards, whose duty it was to stand guard in the court and at palace entrances; the guards outside the palace; and the garrison troops of the capital. The function of the latter was to protect the capital and to make expeditions at the order of the emperor. Judging from the position of the pits and the infantrymen, cavalrymen, and chariots they contained, they probably represented the troops stationed just outside the city. Those in Pit No. 1 form the right wing, those in Pit No. 2, the left wing. Pit No. 3 is the command unit. Warriors in the abandoned Pit No. 4 probably represented the central army. The pits themselves look like armed camps, with large numbers of infantrymen, cavalrymen, and chariots in combat readiness for any eventuality.

The pits under excavation are only a small part of the total peripheral area of the mausoleum. These works attract keen attention from historians, archeologists, sculptors, art historians, military scientists, and weapons experts. Recent exploration to the west of the mausoleum has unearthed painted bronze sculptures, slightly under lifesize, of two four-horse chariots and their drivers. To the endless streams of visitors, all these amazing objects created over 2,000 years ago hold no end of wonder.

125. Inside the museum. The arched building stretches 660 feet from east to west, and 228 feet north to south; height is 72 feet; it covers more than 1 1/2 square miles. The roof turns the entire excavation into a unique *in situ* museum

5. The Han Tombs at Mawangdui, Changsha: Underground Home of an Aristocratic Family

Prince Ma and Marquis Da

Some two miles east of Changsha are two earth mounds, now in the Dongdundu Commune. The mounds were believed to be the family graveyard of Prince Ma Yin of Chu, of the Five Dynasties Period (907–970), and the place became known as Mawangdui (mounds of Prince Ma).

In 1952 archeologists from the Chinese Academy of Sciences discovered that the mounds are of approximately the same size—52 feet high, the bottom diameter 131 feet, and that of the flat top 98 feet. After studying data from their investigation, they concluded that the tombs were more than one thousand years earlier, actually of the Western Han Dynasty (206 B.C.–24 A.D.). Mawangdui was placed under the protection of the government of Hunan Province.

Toward the end of 1971 a hospital project was started nearby, and the eastern mound lay within the work area. The Provincial Museum sent people to work there for three months. These archeologists made the remarkable discovery of what has become known as Tomb No. 1. To their immense surprise they found a burial chamber, well sealed with white clay and charcoal, and within it a decorated wooden coffin containing two smaller coffins, each encased also with clay and charcoal. On top of the innermost coffin was a T-shaped cover of painted silk. Inside, the corpse was female, and intact; textiles and clothing were in good condition; the colors of the lacquerware were fresh and shining. There were wooden figures, musical instruments, pottery, and even some food; the T-shaped cover of the inner coffin was a complete silk painting, or banner; utensils of woven bamboo were found, and bamboo strips bearing a list of the burial objects.

On the bamboo utensils there are clay seals of "Household Manager of Marquis Da" and the lacquerware bears inscriptions of "Family of Marquis Da"; evidently the tomb belonged to a member of the Da family. In the *Historical Records* it says, "The state of Da has 700 households. In the second year of the rule of Hui Di of the Han [193 B.C.], Li Cang, prime minister of Changsha, was granted the marquis . . ." This state-

All works illustrated in this chapter are in the Hunan Provincial Museum, Changsha

127. Model of Tomb No. 1. The burial chamber is at the bottom, and paved with a layer of white clay 6″ thick. Tightly packed against the top and the four sides of the outer coffin are quantities of charcoal, a layer 15–19″ thick and weighing five tons. Between the top red clay and the charcoal is another layer of white clay 3–4 feet thick. The total depth, from top of the mound to the floor of the chamber, is 65 1/2 feet

126. (*opposite*) Yellowish-brown pongee with "Chengyun" (cloud) patterns

128. Excavation site of Tomb No. 1

129. The pit, Tomb No. 1

130. (*opposite*) Tomb No. 1 as discovered. The coffins are in the center with burial objects around them

131. The black coffin with color painting, as it was found. The boards stacked around were from outer coffins

132. The sides of the black painted coffin with cloud patterns dotted with legendary birds and animals. The cover and the sides are decorated with geometrical designs

133. One end of the black painted coffin

134. Dragons, tigers, birds, deer, and "immortals" are painted in bright colors on the red coffin. Designs on one of the ends

130

131

132

133

134

135. The body of the woman lay in four layers of coffins. A black one was on the outside and next to it were, left to right, the black coffin with color paintings (100″ long), the red coffin with color paintings (90″ long) and the beautifully decorated inner coffin (79″ long). All the coffins were painted red inside

ment corresponds to that inscribed on the burial objects, but the title, Marquis of Da, had been bequeathed to three succeeding generations. To which generation did this tomb belong?

From winter 1973 until spring 1974 archeologists worked on the other two tombs (No. 2 and No. 3). In all, more than 1,000 relics were found—books copied on silk, silk paintings, lacquerware, bamboo strips, weapons, musical instruments, and silk fabrics.

Tomb No. 2 was not tightly sealed. It had been robbed several times, and the burial objects remaining inside were damaged. But three seals were intact: "The Seal of Marquis Da," "Prime Minister of Changsha," and "Li Cang." These establish Tomb No. 2 as belonging to the first Marquis of Da. Tombs No. 1 and No. 2 stand side by side, and the mounds are of the same

size; this is a husband-and-wife tomb with two pits, and Tomb No. 1 must belong to Li Cang's wife.

Tomb No. 3 lies south of Tomb No. 1, i.e., at the wife's feet. On a wooden tablet in Tomb No. 3 is an inscription that the burial was in the twelfth year of the reign of Wen Di of the Han, thus 168 B.C. The woman in Tomb No. 1 was about 50 years old; Tomb No. 3 belongs to a man who was over 30; therefore it is not unreasonable to suggest that they were mother and son. But the second Marquis of Da, Li Xi, died in the fifteenth year of Wen Di's rule. That means the owner of Tomb No. 3 was Li Xi's younger brother. Tombs No. 2 and No. 3 are older than Tomb No. 1. The wife died after her husband, and probably after her son.

The owner of Mawangdui was not the Prince of Ma, of the

136. Three seals unearthed from Tomb No. 2 that read: "The Seal of Marquis Da," "Prime Minister of Changsha," and "Li Cang"

141. (*opposite*) Yellow damask (fragment) with "Chengyun" (cloud) patterns

tenth century A.D., but the Marquis of Da, of the second century B.C. The tombs constitute an underground museum displaying the family life of an aristocrat of the Western Han Dynasty.

Silk Fabrics and Lacquerware

Silks and lacquerware were exclusive possessions of the nobility during the second century B.C. China was the first country to breed silkworms and to weave silk fabrics from their cocoons. By the early Han Dynasty, the weaving technique had evidently reached a high level. In Tomb No. 1 were discovered forty-six rolls of woven silk, in addition to lined and unlined dresses, skirts, pillows with cases, gloves, socks, and shoes, all made of silk fabrics. Fifty-eight dresses and other articles were preserved in good condition. These silks were of different kinds—plain tough silk, silk gauze, plain-color damask, and colorful brocade.

The white tough silk was in greatest quantity, the finer weaves (200 warps per inch) used to make robes, while the coarser ones (100 warps per inch) were used for linings and for making skirts and socks. Gauze was of two types, printed and painted. In quality it was better than the tough silk, and it was used for

137. Red gauze with lozenge pattern
138. Fragment of red pongee with "Changshou" pattern
139. Beige pongee with "Xinqi" patterns
140. Fragment of yellow pongee with "Changshou" (longevity) pattern

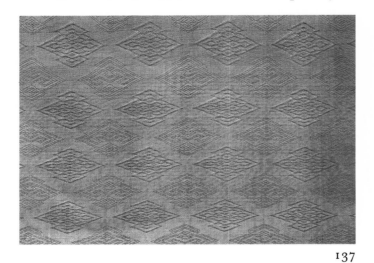

137

138

139

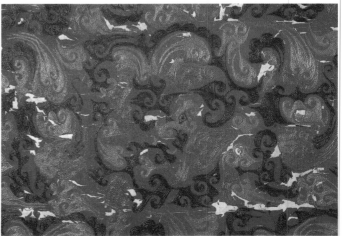

140

142. Heavy silk with rhombic design, pasted with down

143. Embroidered brocade

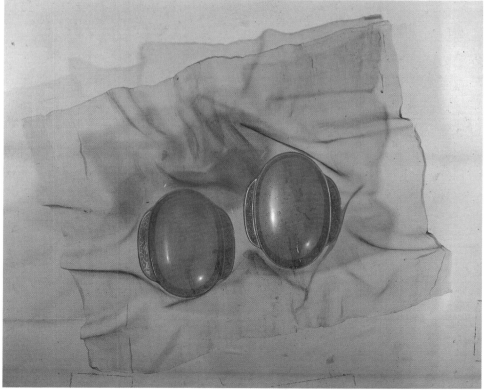

144. Lacquer wine cups seen through
transparent gauze

145. Padded robe in deep red silk with
     color patterns. Length 52″

146. Dark reddish-purple skirt

147. Robe of plain gauze. Length 50 3/8'';
weight 1.5 oz.

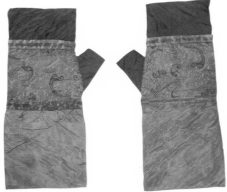

148. Embroidered gloves with "Xinqi"
patterns. Length 9 3/4''

149. Silk shoes. Length 9 3/8''

sheer, unlined garments as well as for the outside of lined robes. The damask was of good quality, and used for robes, bags of fragrant herbs, and gloves, among the articles found. But the best of the Han textiles were the brocades, used for the decorative borders of garments.

Silk embroidery thread in twenty colors was found in the tomb. Forty of the dresses and other articles were embroidered, the patterns geometric in form, or of plants and flowers. Traces of drawing were visible on a number of garments.

Silks and dresses of the Han Dynasty have already been discovered in the northern provinces—Xinjiang, Gansu, and Inner Mongolia—but most of these are later in date, belonging to late Western Han and to the Eastern Han (25–220 A.D.). The Mawangdui relics are the earliest known from the early Western Han Dynasty, and these gauzes, damasks, and brocades already show an accomplished level of silk weaving. The printed and painted silks, too, are high achievements in the arts of printing and dyeing textiles.

The owners of the Mawangdui tombs were buried between 160 and 150 B.C., not long after the founding of the Western Han in 206 B.C. The fabrics are evidence that silk textile techniques continued to develop during the tumultuous centuries including the Warring States Period (475 B.C.–221 B.C.), the unification of the whole country by the Qin (221 B.C.–210 B.C.), and the war

150. Lacquer mug with cloud patterns (without lid, 3 1/2″ high and 3 3/4″ in diameter); lacquer mug with carved cloud and animal patterns (overall height 4 3/8″, diameter 3 1/2″)

151. Lacquer square container with cloud patterns. Overall height 20 1/4″, circumference of mouth 5 7/8″

99

152. Lacquer case with phoenix design.
Overall height 7 1/2″, diameter 8 1/2″

153. Lacquer tray with cloud and dragon
patterns. Diameter 21″

154. Small lacquer tray with cloud and dragon patterns. Diameter 7 1/4″

155. Lacquer tray, plates, cup, and mugs with cloud patterns. Height of tray 2″, length 23 3/4″, width 15 1/2″

156. Lacquer box (diameter
13 1/2″), toilet set, and
bronze mirror

157. (*overleaf*) Lacquer ladles.
Length 16–24″

158. Lacquer round container with cloud
patterns. Overall height 22 3/8'',
diameter 7''

between the Chu and the Han (209 B.C.–206 B.C.). Early in the Han Dynasty some government-run silk mills catered to the needs of the royal families and their aristocrats, whereas in the country the farmer tilled the land while his wife took to the loom. Silks were an important commodity among handicraft articles: a skein of silk yarn or a bolt of silk fabric was usually recognized as a medium of exchange, and high-quality textiles were equivalent to thousands of coins.

Lacquer tripods, cases, bells, square bottles, basins, tables, drinking cups, ladles, dressing cases, and screens were found in

159. Lacquer tripod with cloud patterns. Overall height 11″, diameter 9″

160. Embroidery patterns found in
Tomb No. 1: a) "Xinqi" and flowers;
b) "Changshou" or longevity No. 1;
c) "Changshou" or longevity No. 2;
d) "Chengyun" or clouds

Tombs No. 1 and No. 3, totaling sixteen kinds of objects. Most are decorated with patterns on a black ground—some in red, reddish brown, and grayish green, some in black on a red ground, and some in cinnabar or green pigments. The designs are geometrically proportioned cloud patterns, rings, and rhombuses, or dragons and phoenixes, clouds and birds, flowers and grass, or cats and turtles. They are rich in color and exquisitely produced, with bold and flowing lines. As works of art they have great value.

Lacquerware first appeared late in the Spring and Autumn Period (770 B.C.–476 B.C.). It gradually replaced pottery and bronze vessels in daily use, especially among the aristocracy. Widely used during the Warring States Period—many Warring States lacquer articles have been discovered—lacquerware remained fashionable during the Western Han. An emperor gave lacquerware to his officials in acknowledgment of services. Lacquer articles required a fine and complicated technique and became even more valuable than bronzes.

Paintings on Silk

The T-shaped silk painting, sometimes called a banner, that was draped over the inner coffin of the woman is of fine and stiff texture, a single layer brownish yellow in color. The overall length is 6 feet 8 inches, excluding the four tassels.

In the upper, horizontal part of the painting are the sun and moon, two flying dragons, and the snake-tailed demigod. The sun is on the right, and in it is a golden bird. Below is a fusain tree,[1] with eight small suns among its leaves and branches. On the left is the crescent moon, the toad and the rabbit within its horns. Above the left dragon, a lady ascends toward the moon. All of this follows the well-known fairy tale, and the lady who is flying to the moon is probably Chang E.[2]

Two pillars form an entrance at the bottom of the horizontal section: a leopard perches on either pillar, and two well-dressed doorkeepers are seated inside the pillars. Above them are legendary animals and cranes (or wild geese), and on either side of the picture is a huge dragon emitting fire. In *Calling Back the Soul* of "Songs of the Chu"[3] there is mention of "Nine gates of tigers and leopards," meaning that Heaven has nine gates, each guarded by gods, tigers, and leopards. This portion of the paint-

[1] A kind of tree in the fairy tale of Chang E.
[2] Chang E steals the elixir from her husband Hou Yi. After taking the medicine, she flies to the moon.
[3] "Songs of the Chu" is a compilation of the songs and poems of the State of Chu during the Warring States Period. *Calling Back the Soul*, one of its chapters, was written by Qu Yuan when he was in deep sorrow over the death of Prince Huai of Chu as a prisoner in the State of Qin.

161. Detail of Tomb No. 1 silk painting (upper part)

162. Detail of Tomb No. 1 silk painting (middle part)

163. Diagram of silk painting

164. Color silk painting from Tomb No. 1. Length 6′ 8 1/2″

109

165. Color silk painting from Tomb No. 3. Its contents are similar to those of the Tomb No. 1 painting. Length 7′ 7″

166, 167. Detail of upper part of the silk
painting from Tomb No. 3

168. Detail of middle part of the silk
painting from Tomb No. 3

169. Lower part of the silk painting from
Tomb No. 3

ing probably describes the "Heavenly Gates," and beyond them is the "Heavenly Kingdom," the aristocrats' paradise after death.

In the vertical portion below, two tall dragons pass through a huge round piece of jade carved with patterns of millet grains. The jade separates this portion into two parts, upper and lower. In the upper part, an old lady in the center is leaning on a stick. On her left are two men holding trays and on her right, three attending maids. She wears a long hairpin with a string of white beads hanging in front of her forehead, symbolic of her high social position. The platform underneath the group is supported on a

170. Rectangular silk painting from the western chamber wall of Tomb No. 3, depicting a guard of honor of horsemen and chariots. Length about 7'

slanting board, with a red leopard on either side. High overhead is a canopy with two red birds and a flower in the center, and beneath the canopy is a fantastic winged creature. This section can be construed as the human world. The old lady is the owner of the tomb, and the skirts and robes worn by the group are a true reflection of the actual finds in the tomb.

In the lower half a heavy curtain is parted to reveal the commencement of a feast or sacrificial ceremony. Seven seated men are facing each other on a platform, with pots of food at the front and a dining table in the rear. The platform rests on a giant

171, 172. Details from rectangular silk painting
from Tomb No. 3

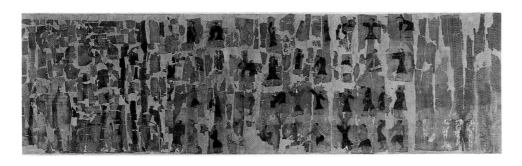

173. Silk painting stored in a lacquer box with the medical treatises; depicts figures sitting calmly, stretching their arms, bending their knees, clasping their legs, and squatting. Positions are closely related to the medical treatises, of which they may be illustrations

174. Detail of painting

who rides on a snake. Beneath the snake are two big fish, and a turtle carrying an owl on its back climbs up each side, in its mouth a plant with a large glossy leaf. Some people consider this section a representation of the underworld, but no reasonable explanation has yet been found for the giant, the fish, and the turtles.

Tomb No. 3 contained four silk paintings, one of them also T-shaped and placed over the coffin. The overall length is 7 feet 7 inches. The composition is in many ways like the silk painting in Tomb No. 1, with the sun and moon, the fusain tree, the toad, and the rabbit in the upper part. Instead of Chang E, stars appear between the sun and the moon. In the center is a demigoddess with outstretched hand, her lower body in the form of a snake; beside her is a flying man naked to the waist. In the upper part of the center section the owner of the tomb is out walking. The face is damaged, but the figure is evidently that of a man wearing a Han hat and a red robe, with a sword dangling at his waist. He is followed by six attendants, and three men greet him respectfully. Below is another depiction of a feast or sacrificial ceremony, and at the bottom a giant is standing on two large fish.

The subject of both of these paintings is the same: "Leading the Soul to Heaven." This is a reflection of the beliefs of that time. The dragons, snakes, legendary creatures, birds, and fish are all characters in ancient fairy tales.

Another of the four paintings in Tomb No. 3 illustrates a guard of honor in procession. It is partly damaged, but some hundred people, several hundred horses, and dozens of carts are discernible. The fragments of another painting, seriously damaged, show houses, carts, galloping horses, and women in boats, and the scene may have to do with the life of the owner of the tomb.

The last painting was found in a lacquer case. The figures are in several rows, some dressed in long gowns and others in tunics. Some are sitting erect, some stretch their arms over their heads, some pull back their abdomens while inhaling and squatting, some are holding their knees. Together with the lacquer case were bamboo strips inscribed with instructions for deep-breathing exercises. It can be reasonably said that the painting illustrates these exercises for people who wanted to keep fit.

All of the paintings are of utmost value for the study of the life of the aristocracy, and for knowledge of religious beliefs, economy, and culture in the early Western Han Dynasty. As works of art, they are the earliest complete paintings known in China, and important for all students of the history of figure painting. In the Mawangdui paintings the figures are shown either from the front or from the side, a convention characteristic of an early style in painting. The paintings are designed with flowing lines and rich color; the composition is often symmetrical and the figures expressive.

Books, Bamboo Strips, and Maps

Before the invention of paper sometime during the Eastern Han Dynasty, writings were inscribed on bamboo strips or written on silk fabrics. These constituted the ancient Chinese books.

Most of the bamboo strips found in Tomb No. 1 carried lists of funerary objects. Two hundred strips from Tomb No. 3 were probably strung together to form a medical treatise in a style similar to *Huang Di Nei Jing* ("The Yellow Emperor's Classic of Internal Medicine"), China's oldest medical work, and thought to be related to *Huang Di Wai Jing* ("The Yellow Emperor's

175. Fragments of the *Book of Changes.* The plain-woven silk is some 20″ wide. Characters are written vertically and are lined with cinnabar. Apart from a few seal characters, the calligraphy is mostly in the clerical form of the style of early Qin. This was the official writing during Emperor Wen Di's reign. Books copied on silk made their first appearance in the Western Zhou Dynasty (11th century B.C.–771 B.C.)

Classic of External Medicine"), of which the title is known but no copy has yet been found.

The books on silk discovered in Tomb No. 3 amount to 120,000 characters, an unprecedented find in the annals of Chinese archeology. More than twenty titles in all, the majority of these are copies of books long considered lost. They include Version A of *Lao Zi*, having four untitled essays at the end; Version B of *Lao Zi*, with *Jing Fa, Shi Da Jing, Cheng,* and *Dao Yuan* at the beginning, as well as *I Ching* (the *Book of Changes*), *Yi Shuo* (Notes to the *Book of Changes*), and *Zhan Guo Ce* (*Records of the Warring States*). There are also books on astronomy, calendar-making, the five elements, the appearance of horses, and astrology. In addition, there are two maps of a region with mountains, rivers, and roads, of which more below.

Lao Zi is also known as *Dao De Jing*, the classic text of the Taoists. Lao Zi's teachings exerted a profound influence on Chinese philosophy. The two versions of *Lao Zi* found at Mawangdui share more or less the same contents. Compared with the extant edition, the two texts differ in many places. The first of the four untitled essays of Version A is written in a style similar to that of *Da Xue* (*The Great Learning*),[4] and advocates the teaching of Confucius. The second essay quotes Yi Yin on how to rule the country.[5] The "Annals of Yin" of the *Historical Records* says that Yi Yin talked with King Tang of "Prince Su and the nine categories of princes"; it is recorded in the *Yi Wen Zhi*[6] of the *Chronicles of the Han Dynasty* that Yi Yin had written fifty-one essays, but all were lost. Therefore the discovery of this quotation is important. The third essay discusses tactics of attack and defense. The fourth deals with the five elements[7] and the relations among morality, divinity, and wisdom; this essay has been greatly damaged and the text cannot be understood.

Version B, with *Jing Fa, Shi Da Jing, Cheng,* and *Dao Yuan* at the beginning, has a total of 11,164 characters. Written during the Warring States Period or the Qin Dynasty, the text is in

176. Fragments of Version B of *Lao Zi*. There are Versions A and B of the 5,000-character *Lao Zi* copied on silk. The order of parts one and two in both editions is opposite to that of the extant versions and the texts differ in some places. Version A was copied during Emperor Hui Di's and Empress Dowager Lu's reign (194 B.C.–180 B.C.); Version B about 179 B.C., the first year of Wen Di's reign

4 One of the Confucian classics. It is of the Qin or Han Period, and in the Song Dynasty it became one of the Four Books, the other three being the *Analects, Mencius,* and the *Golden Mean. The Great Learning* discusses the study of natural phenomena, the attainment of knowledge, sincerity, the right place of the heart, self-cultivation, good family, the ruling of a country, and the peaceful unification of the world.

5 A high official of the early Shang Dynasty (16th century B.C.—11th century B.C.) who helped Tang to overthrow Jie of Xia and ruled over the country. Yi is the name; Yin is the official title.

6 The *Chronicles of the Han Dynasty* is China's first dynastic historical text. It was written by Ban Gu of the Eastern Han. *Yi Wen Zhi* is a book catalogue.

7 Referring to metal, wood, water, fire, and earth: ancient Chinese thinkers used the five elements as a means to explain the origin of all things in the world, and the unification of diversity.

177. At the end of Version A of *Lao Zi* are four previously lost and untitled essays; at the beginning of Version B are *Jing Fa* and three other previously lost essays. Pictured here is part of *Jing Fa*

good condition. Some maintain that these four articles are none other than the "Four Classics of the Yellow Emperor" listed in the *Yi Wen Zhi*. The Yellow Emperor and Lao Zi were both held in high esteem during the reign of Wen Di of Han,[8] which explains why their writings were bound together. *Jing Fa* advocates legalism; it considers important the rule of the country by law. *Shi Da Jing* records deeds of the Yellow Emperor and his officials, and discourses among them. Some consider it to be the "Yellow Emperor and His Officials" named in the *Yi Wen Zhi*. *Cheng* is written in short sentences like mottoes; it advocates fatalism. *Dao Yuan* is a Taoist treatise, dealing with the origin of Dao (The Way).

The *Book of Changes* is one of the Confucian classics. It was thought to be of the Zhou Dynasty, but recent research has shown that its date is either during the Warring States Period or the Qin Dynasty, and that it was written by several authors at different periods. Using the Eight Diagrams (linear symbols of natural powers: heaven, earth, thunder, wind, water, fire, mountain, and lake), it expounds changes in nature and, symbolically, in society. It maintains the origin of all things as the interaction of *yin* (feminine and negative) and *yang* (masculine and positive). This recently excavated version of the *Book of Changes* is untitled, and has about 5,200 characters. Three articles at the end serve as notes to the text.

Zhan Guo Ce is a compilation of memorials and speeches made by scholars on proselytizing missions among the Warring States. The edition by Liu Xiang, scholar of Western Han (77 B.C.–6 B.C.), contains thirty-three articles, but some of these were lost during the Song Dynasty (960–1279 A.D.). Twenty-eight excavated articles, totaling 11,200 characters, are related to *Zhan Guo Ce*; though none has a title, they are speeches and memorials of Su Qin, Su Dai, Su Li, Tian Ying, and Li Dui, all advisers of the Warring States Period. Eleven of the articles occur in the extant version, but the texts have notable differences.

There are essays on historical facts of the *Spring and Autumn Annals* by Zuoqiu Ming. These are not in chronological order; some facts coincide with those of Zuoqiu Ming, but reflect a different point of view, and some of the items are not recorded in the *Spring and Autumn Annals*. A classic of the Confucian school, the *Annals* are based on the history of the various states during the Spring and Autumn Period (770 B.C.–476 B.C.).

In addition to these classical treatises, there are works on

[8] In early Han, the Yellow Emperor and Lao Zi were respected as the founders of Taoism. After the peasants' uprisings at the end of the Qin Dynasty, Emperor Wen Di of Han adopted restorative policies to enable the people to live peacefully and increase production.

178. Fragments of Version A of *Lao Zi*

179. Excavated books on astronomy, formerly lost, of some 6,000 characters record achievements made in early Western Han Dynasty

180. The excavated manuscript of *Zhan Guo Ce* ("Records of the Warring States") has 12,000 characters in 28 chapters. Eighteen of the chapters, none known before, record activities of diplomats Su Qin, Su Dai, Li Dui, and other statesmen. In this picture: Fragments of *Zhan Guo Ce*, recording Chu Long's interview with the Queen Dowager of Zhao. Chu Long advised the queen to stop spoiling her children, and to encourage them to serve their country. Chu Long is mentioned in the *Historical Records*; he is named Chu Zhe in the extant edition of *Zhan Guo Ce*

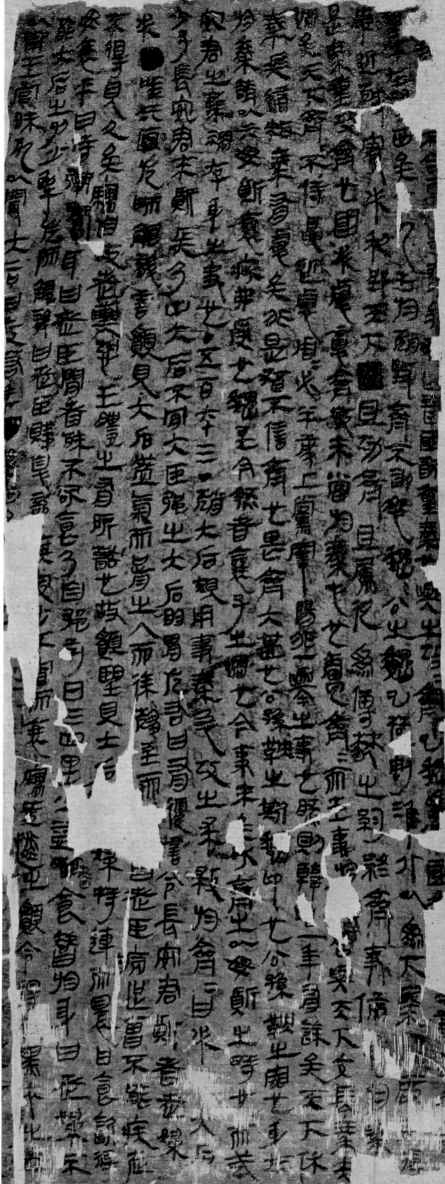

astronomy and astrology, among them records of the motion of the five planets—Venus, Jupiter, Mercury, Mars, and Saturn—in the 70 years between the accession of the First Emperor of Qin (246 B.C.) and the third year of Wen Di of Han (177 B.C.). From these data was calculated the time needed for each planet to journey around the sun. It is recorded, for instance, that the planet known as Saturn requires thirty years to make its circuit, a finding very close to the actual time of 29.46 years. These are the earliest known works of Chinese astronomical literature.

The medical treatise records several hundred prescriptions, as well as the causes of diseases and their symptoms. The maps and charts show the disposition of garrison forces, and include mountains, rivers, cities and towns, and roads. The area covered

181. In Tomb No. 3 were found two maps marked with mountains, rivers, cities, towns, and roads. One shows military posts, numbers of households in villages, and the distance between them. These are the earliest maps yet discovered in China. Together with the funerary weapons found here, these maps suggest that the occupant of this tomb might have been a military officer

182. The map showing the disposition of troops
183. Detail of map

by one map lies in southern Hunan, northeast Guangzi, and northern Guangdong. The military disposition map shows places of garrisons, cities and castles, villages, including size of population and distances between them, and the course of the mountains. These are the earliest Chinese maps ever discovered.

A large number of the silk books deal with the politics, military affairs, ideology, culture, science, and technology of early Western Han. Some of these have not only been lost to us in the present era but also were unknown to Liu Xiang and Ban Gu, the writer and historian of the Eastern Han Dynasty (39–92 A.D.). Such is the overwhelming importance of this find.

The Woman in Tomb No. 1

There remains to be discussed the body of the woman. She wore many dresses and lay beneath twenty quilts. As the covers and dresses were removed one after another, everyone was astonished to see that the body was in perfect condition with no sign of decomposition.

The woman is five feet tall, and weighs 75 1/2 pounds. The brownish-yellow skin is smooth and resilient, and the facial features are distinct. The body is in good condition and the internal organs are intact, as are the veins and arteries. Physiological tests have shown that she had several kinds of disease: the left coronary artery was almost closed; she had atherosclerosis in several parts of her body; and she had a serious and frequently recurring case of gallstones—one of the two largest stones was lodged at the end of the main gallbladder duct, the other one was in the liver duct. She was about fifty years old, had plenty of fat, and no sign of bedsores. She evidently died of an acute illness, probably a coronary attack caused by pain in the gallbladder. In her esophagus, stomach, and intestines there are still 138.5 melon seeds; she had been eating melon shortly before she died.

It is generally agreed that the tightly sealed chamber and the layers of charcoal and white clay outside the multiple coffins explain the extraordinary preservation of this deeply buried body

184. The neatly wrapped body when discovered
185. The body of the woman. Height 60″

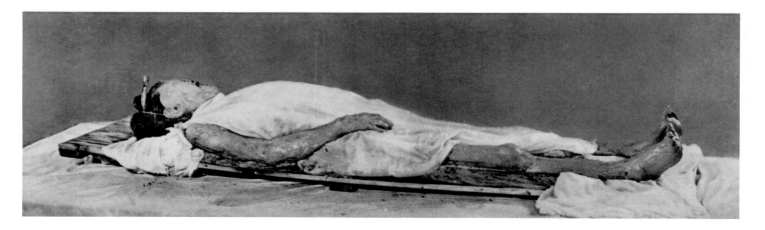

186. Crowned and costumed male figurine. Height 30″

187. Painted figurines playing musical instruments. Heights 12–15″

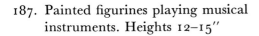

for more than 2,100 years. The temperature remained low, little oxygen was admitted, and the inside of the coffin was free of bacteria. These circumstances are rare in human history.

The Wooden Figures

After the turbulence of the downfall of the Qin Dynasty, the Western Han government adopted a policy of restoration. Emperor Wen Di advocated a thrifty and simple life. It was prohibited to bury gold, silver, bronze, or tin with the dead: thus none of these metals occurs in the Mawangdui tombs. The funerary objects nevertheless demonstrate fully a luxurious life for the deceased. The great number of wooden figures—dancing girls, musicians, and ladies-in-waiting—remind us of the slaves, men as well as girls, and of the cattle, sheep, houses, and crop fields of the rich. The food of the time is evident in great variety—rice, wheat, broomcorn millet, and millet; pears, dates, plums, and red bayberries; hare, dog, pork, venison, beef, and mutton; wild goose, duck, chicken, pheasant, turtledove, sparrow, and crane; carp, crucian carp, bream, and mandarin fish; and condiments such as sweetgrass, osmanthus, and honey.

Changsha, still a famous city south of the Changjiang River, belonged during the Warring States Period to the State of Chu. At the beginning of the Han Dynasty it was a state with thirteen counties under its jurisdiction, situated in the middle and lower reaches of the Zishui and Xiangjiang rivers. The *Historical Records* mentions this area as vast in size but sparse in population: "No one dies of cold and hunger. No one has one thousand ounces of gold." It is clear that the area was not yet well developed, and economically backward.

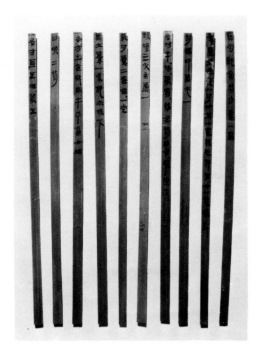

Da County of the Han is in the vicinity of present-day Guangshan in Henan. Marquis Da had but 700 households. But Li Cang, the first Marquis of Da, was an emissary of the emperor supervising the Prince of Changsha, and Marquis Da had, in addition to 700 households, the 25,000 households of the State of Changsha as well. His was really a family of "one thousand ounces of gold."

Although hundreds of Han tombs have been discovered, thus far the Mawangdui tombs are the best preserved. The family of Marquis Da built the tombs before they died in order to continue their luxurious life after death. They could never have dreamed that one day all this would become valuable material for scholars in many branches of learning.

188. Bamboo container with eggs
189. Bamboo strips from Tomb No. 1 listing burial accessories
190. Pears

6. Two Tombs of Zhongshan and Their Rare Jade Burial Suits

In the southwestern section of Mancheng County, Hebei Province, there is a limestone mountain about 650 feet high called Lingshan ("mountain of the mausoleum"). Not far from Lingshan Mountain there is a little village called Shouling ("guard the mausoleum"). No one knows when the village was named, but the tombs of China's emperors in ancient times were called Ling. Since the mountain is called Lingshan and Shouling village is near it, could the tomb of an ancient emperor be found close by?

In the summer of 1968 a unit of the People's Liberation Army was carrying out a construction project in the area, and they discovered a large artificial cave that contained many bronze vessels, earthenware, and articles of iron and jade. The P.L.A. men stopped digging and reported their find to the appropriate department, meanwhile guarding the site. An archeological team soon arrived. While sorting out the historical relics in the cave, which the archeologists determined was a tomb, they discovered that the mountain slope at the entrance was littered with chips of rock evidently left from digging the tomb out of the mountain. More rock chips were found not far away, suggesting the presence of another tomb. A trial excavation led to the discovery of the second tomb, and the secret of Lingshan, the name of the mountain, was revealed.

All works illustrated in this chapter are in the Hebei Provincial Museum, Shijiazhuang

191. Inlaid gilt-bronze vessel. Height of wine container 17″. There are several gold-and-silver-plated rings on the body of the vessel. Gold-plated slanting patterns form rhombuses and triangles inlaid with green glaze. At the many cross points are silver knobs

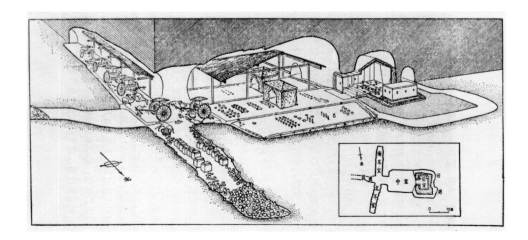

192. Sketch map of Liu Sheng's tomb. Behind the entrance of the tomb is a 65-foot-long underground passage. The south chamber at the end of the passage is a room for chariots and horses and the north chamber is a storehouse for foodstuffs and wine. The central chamber is a square hall in which a variety of articles of bronze, iron, lacquerware, gold, and silver, as well as many pottery and stone figurines symbolizing servants, were all placed in an orderly way. Beyond a white marble door is the rear chamber, symbolizing a bedroom, in which the coffin was placed

193. Pottery wine-containers and vessels in the storehouse of Dou Wan's tomb

194. The central chamber of Liu Sheng's tomb viewed from the entrance of the underground passage

Immense Tombs

Both tombs, though carved out of solid rock, are very large: they are literally underground palaces. The maximum dimensions of Tomb No. 1 are 170 feet long, 121 feet wide, and nearly 23 feet high. The cubic space in Tomb No. 2 is even larger.

The two tombs are similar in shape and structure. Each includes an entrance passage, two side chambers on the south and north, a central chamber, and a rear chamber. The underground passage leading to the central chamber is 65 feet long. The south chamber, just before the end of the passage, was for chariots and horses; the north chamber was a storehouse where wine containers were placed, and vessels and jars for grain, fish, and meat. In addition, cooking utensils and tableware, such as tripods, cauldrons, cups, and plates, were also found there.

The central chamber consisted of a great hall in which a variety of bronze vessels, lacquerware, and earthenware were placed in an orderly way, as well as many figurines made of pottery and stone. The hall, about 50 feet long by 40 feet wide, was built of wood within the rock cave; the wooden structure might have been very magnificent, but it has decayed and collapsed.

A white marble door closes off the central chamber from the rear chamber. The rear chamber has two rooms, the larger a stone room 16 by 13 feet, its walls painted with red lacquer. In the north of the room was a white marble bed on which the coffin was placed. The coffin had collapsed but the jade burial suit sewn with gold thread which shrouded the remains of the deceased is well preserved. At the south of the room is a bathroom containing a basin, jar, lamp, and incense burner, and a stone for rubdowns together with a stone figurine symbolizing a manservant.

Whose Tombs Are These?

When were these tombs built? Who was buried in them? Judging by the form of the tombs and the funerary objects found there, archeologists confirmed that they belonged to the period of the Western Han Dynasty (206 B.C.–24 A.D.): many bronze articles in the tombs are inscribed with the words "Zhongshan Principality," and the corpses are shrouded in jade burial suits sewn with gold thread, a custom observed only by Han emperors and high-ranking aristocrats. Mancheng was the seat of the Principality of Zhongshan during the Western Han Dynasty, a fact which further confirmed for archeologists the identity of the tombs. According to historical data, there were six princes in the Principality of Zhongshan: which prince, then, was buried here?

Archeologists found that in some of the inscriptions on the funerary bronze objects there were "reign titles," and that these records covered some thirty years. Every emperor or prince who ascended the throne in ancient China had his own reign title, and of the six princes in the Zhongshan Principality, only the reign of Liu Sheng, Prince Jing of Zhongshan, lasted over thirty years. The archeologists concluded that the tombs are those of Liu Sheng, Prince Jing of Zhongshan of the Western Han Dynasty, and of his wife, Dou Wan.

The feudal system of enfeoffment was practiced in the earlier years of the Western Han Dynasty. Except for the crown prince, most of the emperor's sons would be made princes. Liu Sheng's mother was a concubine of Liu Qi, Emperor Jing Di (154 B.C.– 141 B.C.). Liu Sheng was made Prince Jing of the Zhongshan Principality in 154 B.C., during the reign of his father, Emperor Jing Di. Liu Sheng died in 113 B.C., during the reign of Emperor Wu Di, and was on the throne of the Principality for forty-two years. There were more than 160,000 households in the Principality of Zhongshan at the time, with a population of 668,000 people.

First Well-Preserved Jade Burial Suits

195, 196. (*above and below*) Well-preserved jade burial suits tied with gold thread, first of their kind ever found in China, unearthed in the tombs of Liu Sheng and Dou Wan. Jade burial suits were reserved for emperors and aristocrats in feudal China, and were prevalent during the Western Han Dynasty. The suits are made of jade wafers of different shapes tied with gold, silver, or bronze thread

Jade burial suits are made of pieces of jade tied together. The custom prevailed during the Western Han Dynasty, based on the people's belief that the suit would keep the corpse from decomposing. By the subsequent Eastern Han Dynasty, jade suits were made according to rigid rules: emperors were buried in jade suits tied with gold thread, princesses in suits tied with silver thread, and the concubines and sisters of the emperors in suits tied with bronze thread. The custom continued to the end of the dynasty. In the following period, the Three Kingdoms, Emperor Wen Di of the Wei Kingdom (220–265 A.D.) gave orders forbidding the use of suits of jade for burials, saying that it was a foolish custom. From then on jade burial suits were used no more.

China's history books contain many records of jade burial suits, but no examples in good condition had been found before. The two perfectly preserved jade suits, both tied with gold thread, that were unearthed in the tombs of Liu Sheng and his wife, Dou Wan, are the first of their kind ever discovered.

Liu Sheng's jade suit, 74 inches long, is made of 2,498 pieces of jade; that of Dou Wan is smaller, 67 3/4 inches long, and composed of 2,160 pieces of jade. The pieces are designed in different sizes and shapes according to the parts of the body they covered; most of them are rectangular wafers, a few are triangular. They are joined with gold thread through tiny holes in the corners of each piece. Liu Sheng's suit is tied with 2 1/2 pounds of gold thread, and Dou Wan's with 1 1/4 pounds; the diameter of the

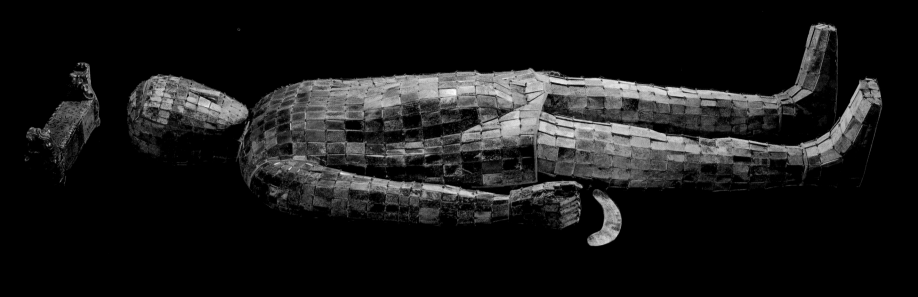

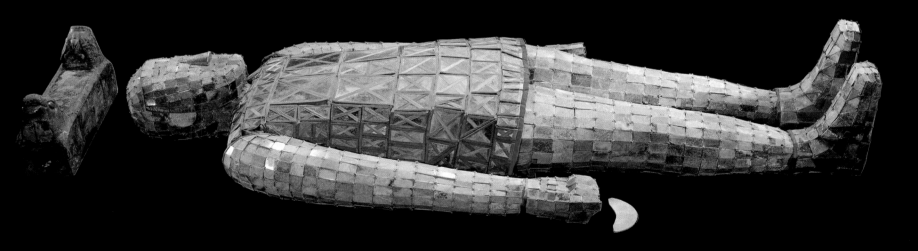

finest thread is 0.08–0.13 millimeter, which shows the prime workmanship 2,000 years ago in the technique of drawing wire. Each jade suit consists of five parts: mask, jacket, trousers, gloves, and shoes; these are composed of several smaller parts for convenience in dressing the deceased. Assembled, the jade suit looks like the body of a person. In the experience of a present-day jadesmith, an expert jadesmith of the Han Dynasty would have needed more than ten years to complete such a suit. The two jade suits indicate the consummate technical skill of these early artisans. Marks on the jade show that it was cut with a very fine saw, only 0.3 millimeter thick. Some of the holes at the corners were bored with a tube-type drill using sand drilling, the holes being only one millimeter in diameter.

Exquisite Bronze Vessels

Over 2,800 objects were discovered in the tombs of Liu Sheng and his wife, Dou Wan, including articles of bronze, gold, silver, jade, iron, pottery, and lacquerware, and silk fabrics. The bronze vessels unearthed are of high technical and artistic quality, with delicate and beautiful designs, and belong among the finest bronze articles of the ancient period. Two examples are the Changxin lamp and the Boshan incense burner.

The Changxin lamp from Dou Wan's tomb is in the shape of a palace maidservant who holds the lamp. The gilded surface of the 19-inch-high lamp is still shining. The girl's hair is put up in a chignon; she wears a long dress with wide sleeves. She holds the lamp with her left hand and raises her right hand, the broad cuff of her sleeve becoming the lampshade. There is a candle-pin in the center of the dish, and the semicircular walls around it are adjustable; by moving the handle, the direction and intensity of the candle's light can be controlled.

Within the maidservant's right arm is a pipe through which the smoke passes into her hollow body, keeping the room smoke-free. The lamp is made in several parts, so it can be taken apart for cleaning.

On nine places on the lamp there are inscriptions, totaling sixty-five words, that indicate the owner of the lamp, the date it was made, and its weight. The lamp once belonged in the Changxin Palace, so it was called the Changxin lamp. Doushi, the grandmother of Liu Sheng, was the queen of Liu Heng, Emperor Wen Di (179 B.C.–157 B.C.), and she lived in the Changxin Palace when she was empress dowager. Doushi had come from Guanjin of Qinghe (now Wuyi County, Hebei Province). Guanjin was near the Zhongshan Principality, and archeologists have inferred that Dou Wan was a relative of someone in the Empress Dowager Doushi's parents' home—it might even be that the lamp was bestowed on Dou Wan in the Changxin Palace by the

197. Changxin lamp from Dou Wan's tomb. Height 19″. The lamp held by the palace maidservant comprises a lamp bowl and a shade. The semicircular lampshade is adjustable: the handle on the left side can be moved to control the direction and intensity of the light. The smoke rises through the right arm of the girl into the hollow body, keeping the room smoke-free

200. (*opposite*) Incense burner from tomb of Liu Sheng. Height 10 1/4″. Bronze, inlaid with gold in an overall pattern. Its lid has the shape of the peaks of an imaginary elfland mountain— Boshan Mountain. It is the most elegant and refined of all the Boshan incense burners thus far discovered

empress dowager. This lamp and eighteen others were unearthed from the tombs of Liu Sheng and Dou Wan. All are beautifully and skillfully designed: the lamp in the shape of a bird has the bird holding the oil pan in its beak; the back of the lamp in the shape of a kneeling ram can be lifted and turned to become the oil pan resting on the ram's head.

The Boshan incense burner is another priceless treasure from Liu Sheng's tomb. Its lid is shaped like a mountain with successive peaks, each having many tiny holes to permit smoke to come out when incense is burned. The mountain peaks symbolize the Taoist myth of Boshan Mountain, on the Isle of the Immortals,

198. Bronze scarlet bird lamp. Height 11″. Ingeniously shaped lamp in the form of a flying bird which holds in its beak a round tripartite dish, so that three wicks could burn at the same time. The scarlet bird was regarded as supernatural in ancient times

199. Lamp in the shape of a kneeling ram. Height 9″. The back becomes an oval-shaped dish when it is lifted and reversed onto the head of the ram. The mouth of the dish held the wick, and the dish contained lamp oil

in the Eastern Sea. The 10-inch-high Boshan incense burner is inlaid with gold in an allover pattern. The fretwork stem has three dragons rising from the surging seas. Their heads support the bowl, which is decorated with inlaid patterns like clouds moving with the wind. On the top are the peaks of Boshan Mountain; tigers and leopards are running among the precipitous peaks, and charming monkeys squat on top of the peaks or play on the backs of the animals; hunters are pursuing a wild boar. This sculptured incense burner has become a lively and beautiful landscape, surely used by an aristocratic owner.

Chariots and Horses in Western Han

In the slave society began the practice of immuring real chariots and horses as funerary sacrifices. Tombs of the Shang Dynasty (c. 16th century B.C.–c. 11th century B.C.) were discovered in Anyang containing sacrificed chariots, horses, and even drivers. In the feudal society it became more customary to use models of chariots and horses as funerary objects for noble burials. But in the tombs of Liu Sheng and his wife, Dou Wan, real chariots and horses were sacrificed: there were six chariots and seventeen horses in Liu Sheng's tomb, four chariots and thirteen horses in Dou Wan's tomb. Buried for 2,000 years, only the skeletons of the horses remained, but the metalwork of the chariots and harnesses was intact, permitting archeologists to restore the wooden chariots to their original form.

Each chariot had two wheels and a single shaft, and was drawn by two, three, or four horses. The chariot is composed of six parts: wheel, axle, yoke, transverse, box, and canopy. Most of the wheels are sixty inches in diameter with twenty-four spokes, and the wheels were about six feet apart. Chariots were made for different purposes: crossbows were placed in the hunting chariot; in the tomb of Dou Wan a small chariot for one person was excavated, its box only three feet wide. It was a special car for a noblewoman to use within the palace grounds.

The tops of the axles and shafts and the two ends of the transverse of the chariots were of bronze, decorated with gold or silver plate. Some of them are inlaid with gold or with agates and turquoise. Judging from the lacquer that remains, the chariots were painted red, and complicated patterns of clouds and rhombus lines were also painted in red, white, green, and brown colors. The chariot boxes must have been a colorful sight!

202. Bronze ornaments of chariots. The gold-plated top of a shaft inlaid with agates and turquoise (left). Axle inlaid with gold and silver (right)

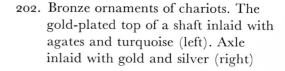

203. Horse skeletons, chariots, harnesses in the south chamber of Liu Sheng's tomb

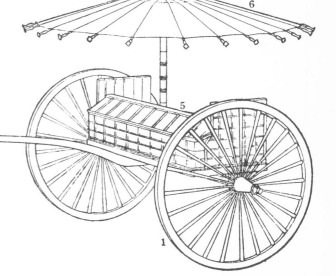

204. Restoration of the chariot in Liu Sheng's tomb: 1) wheel 2) shaft 3) transverse 4) yoke 5) box 6) canopy

201. (*opposite*) Gilt-bronze wine container with gold and silver inlaid patterns. Height 23 1/2″. Four coiled dragons with twin bodies are dancing among the golden clouds

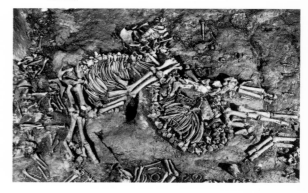

All works illustrated in this chapter are in the Gansu Provincial Museum, Lanzhou

205. "Horse and Swallow". Height 13 1/2″, length 17 3/4″. With hoofs raised high, this vivid image of a fine steed is the embodiment of movement. The startled bird sets off the neighing horse. The whole weight of the horse is cleverly pivoted on the flying swallow

7. "Horse and Swallow": The Bronze Horses of Eastern Han

Hoofs clattering, a spirited horse gallops ahead. It neighs as it steps on a flying swallow in the air. This is the famous Eastern Han bronze unearthed in Wuwei County, Gansu Province.

The precious relic was discovered purely by accident. It was excavated at Leitai, a village of fifty families north of the county seat. Standing on an earth mound at the village entrance is the Temple of the God of Thunder. The ancient Chinese considered wind, rain, thunder, and lightning to be at the will of the gods, each controlled by a different god. Early in 1969 the villagers, while digging foundations, came to an ancient tomb under the earth mound. From it many bronze and jade articles were excavated. The villagers, having no knowledge of the value of these objects, thought they might sell them for money to buy a horse-drawn cart.

Word of the discovery reached a functionary of the county cultural relics administration committee, who went to see the bronzes. Their elegant and exquisite form proved their worth beyond a doubt. This was explained to the villagers, who provided a handcart and sheaves of wheat stalks. The relics were wrapped up in the stalks and trundled off to Wuwei.

The Flying Horse

Over 200 relics were found in Leitai, most of them bronzes, but the excavation had not been carried out professionally and it was impossible to make an official report of it. Judging from the size and shape of the tomb and the style and quality of the funerary objects it contained, it belongs to the Eastern Han Dynasty, 25–220 A.D. An inscription on the chest of one of the bronze horses reveals the owner of the tomb to be one General Zhang. The tomb's three spacious chambers and antechambers are in themselves marks of the owner's power and distinction. The thirty-nine bronze horses and horsemen, the forty-five drivers, escorts, and slaves, and the fourteen chariots must have been drawn up in battle array in recognition of his valiant service.

The horses are strong, powerful, and handsome. The "Flying

206. Leitai, in Wuwei County, Gansu Province. The Eastern Han tomb is under ancient locust trees behind the wall

207. Five bronze horses from the ancient tomb, which contained 39 horses, 1 ox, 14 carts, 20 horsemen, and other escorts. The horses possess the characteristics of the Central Asian or Xinjiang breed: large frame, slender limbs, large hoofs, and short belly

208. Five horsemen of a guard of honor holding spears, halberds, and axes. Average height 21″

209. Two *zhao* carts, each 15″ wide. Two slaves, 9 1/2″ tall, stand at front and back. In elegant taste, a sunshade on top protects the front part of the carriage, covering much of the passenger. The *zhao* cart was used exclusively by generals and noblemen

Horse" is especially fascinating, balanced with one hoof on a swallow with outspread wings. The ancient Chinese praised one species of horse as the "Heavenly Horse," and this unknown artist has created an image that indeed could be of the "Heavenly Horse." The theme of the "Heavenly Horse" is often seen in Chinese paintings, sometimes soaring on two wings into a sky of clouds. Sculpture, however, requires concise design and accurate calculation, with no casual additions for expressive contrasts. Only a great master could have a conception that is at once so bold and logical: the "Horse and Swallow" is an inspired example.

Swallows fly at high speed, and the consummate swiftness of the "Heavenly Horse" is clearly shown by the startled movement of the bird. The artist seems to compare the "lightness" of the horse's movement to that of the swallow. The Chinese like to say, "A body as light as a swallow": a horse, with its heavy body, cannot fly, but here it steps on a swallow in mid-air. This is the artist's image of a "Heavenly Horse."

The reader may ask, "How did this elegant bronze horse come to be made 1,800 years ago, in the Eastern Han Dynasty? Why was it found in the Hexi Corridor?"—a remote region usually thought to be backward culturally.

The answer lies in the "Silk Road." In 178 B.C. the Western Han government (206 B.C.–24 A.D.) sent the traveler Zhang Qian to the Western Region.[1] He blazed a path leading ultimately from Xi'an in the east to Rome in the west, the transcontinental route that later became known as the Silk Road. Precious stones, spices, rare birds, and animals came to the east by this road, and among the latter were fine horses, much needed and coveted by the Han government.

Emperor Wu Di was in particular need of fine horses. The Huns in the north had become strong enough to defeat the Dayuan and Wusun tribes and drive them away from the Hexi Corridor, and thus to harass the Han borders. They looted and kidnaped in the border population. The Han emperors first adopted a policy of appeasement, but it was of no avail. When Wu Di came to the throne (140 B.C.–87 B.C.) he determined to

210. *Da* carts, each 12″ wide. The carriage is rectangular, with a door in the tail board for people and goods. It is a baggage cart for the retinue. The figures are driver slaves and, at the sides, attendant slaves

211. Ox cart. The animal is 8″ high; the cart is 26 3/4″ long in all, and 10″ high. It is similar to the *da* cart in its shape and use

1 In ancient times, China referred to Xinjiang and the land west of it as the Western Region.

212. Gilded *zun*, food container. Height 5″, diameter 9″. This finely worked article must have belonged to a rich family

213. Turtle-shaped stone. Length 12 3/4″, width 10″, height 7 1/2″. Turtles and cranes, because of their long lives, are Chinese symbols of longevity. This stone is one of the four found under the four corners of General Zhang's coffin

stop the Huns by force. Han infantrymen, however, were no match for Hun horsemen. Wu Di required strong cavalry troops, and only in the Western Region could he find good horses for them.

The Emperor sent agents to look for Wusun and Dayuan horses.[2] Jin Midi, a Hun, was appointed head of the thirty-six stables located along the northwestern border, including the Hexi Corridor; he had charge of 300,000 horses, and horse-breeding now became an important branch of husbandry. Alfalfa was introduced to the hinterland to provide good pasturage. The Hexi Corridor, being the throat of the Silk Road, was of strategic importance to the Han government. The Emperor built the Yangguan and Yumen passes in this area and extended the Great Wall to the Yumen. Beacon towers were put up as far as Lop Nur, and many troops were stationed there. Han cavalrymen were often seen on maneuvers in the Hexi Corridor, with bow and arrow or unsheathed saber in hand. "Heavenly Horses" of the Wusun and the Dayuan were much sought after.

Starting with the Western Han Dynasty, more and more people came to the Hexi Corridor from the Central Plain. They possessed a high level of culture and a traditional appreciation of art. The marvelous steeds they saw there left a deep impression on them, which they distilled by their creative imaginations. The living reality sparked the artists' creativity. The inner being of the "Heavenly Horse" emerged in these masterpieces—the "Horse and Swallow," the other bronze horses, and works of art in other mediums.

214. Bronze lamp. Height 3 1/2", diameter 2"

[2] During the Western Han Dynasty, the present-day Ili River and the areas west of it were known as the State of Wusun; the Fergana, now in E. Uzbek S.S.R., was the State of Dayuan. Both regions produced fine horses.

147

8. Culture of the Huns

Recently excavated in the Inner Mongolia Autonomous Region were a number of relics of the Huns, and mural paintings that show the relations of the Huns and other northern peoples with the Hans.

Chinese civilization has developed out of the interflow and merging of the cultures of various nationalities over a long time. Among these cultures, the Huns have played an important part. Hundreds of clans and tribes inhabited China's north during the Spring and Autumn Period and the Warring States Period, from the eighth century B.C. to the third century B.C. Known in Chinese history as "Rong" or "Di," these tribes were distributed north and south of the Gobi Desert, or in the Huang He Valley; others lived scattered among the Hans in central China. Those in the vast Gobi gradually formed themselves into tribal leagues, among these the Huns and the Donghus.

The Huns came originally from the region within the bends of the Huang He and the Yinshan Mountains. The suitable climate and lush pasturage on the vast plain, and the luxuriant forests with plenty of wild animals in the Yinshan Mountains, afforded the early Huns a good life as hunters. Later, as animal husbandry developed and with it the steady need for water and grass, they began to move from place to place. They ate meat, drank milk, wore garments made of animal hide, and lived in yurts. The early Hun tribal leagues varied in size, for they assembled or disbanded from time to time. This way of life lasted for more than 1,000 years, until the reign of Touman Khan in the latter half of the third century B.C., when the tribal league became stabilized. Hun society had evolved from the primitive clan system to the slave system, and the early Hun tribes were producers as well as military units. All able-bodied men practiced hunting and herding animals in peacetime and took up arms in time of war.

Toward the end of the Warring States Period the Chinese principalities were too occupied in fighting one another to attend to the north, and the power of the Hun slave owners increased greatly. In 209 B.C. Touman was slain by his son Maodun, who then proclaimed himself Khan. Seizing the administrative and

All works illustrated in this chapter are in the Museum of the Inner Mongolia Autonomous Region, Hohhot

215. Eagle of gold and turquoise perching on top of a golden crown. Warring States Period. Height 2 1/2″, diameter 3″. From a Hun tomb in Hangjin Banner, Inner Mongolia

military power, Maodun declared the Khan system to be hereditary, and perfected the slave system, thus setting a new page in the history of the Hun.

Maodun conquered the tribes of Donghu in the east, Rouzhi in the west, and Hunyu in the north, and then defeated Loulan and Gusi among twenty-eight other tribes. He forced the newly established Western Han empire to send him large quantities of silks, wine, and rice, in addition to giving him a princess for his bride. The Hun's domain grew swiftly, extending to the Yinshan range in the south, Lake Baikal in the north, Laoha He in the east, and the Pamir Mountains in the west. The first local state power to be unified in China was in the north.

In 140 B.C. Emperor Wu Di of the Han Dynasty had succeeded to the throne. He changed the previous tactics from forbearance and conciliation to armed defense. He launched three major counteroffensives to victory, in 127 B.C., 121 B.C., and 119 B.C., and thereby reduced the strength of the Huns. Nations enslaved by Hun nobles now rose in revolt: Dingling from the north, Wuhuan from the east, Wusun from the west. A heavy fall of snow caused the cattle to freeze and the people to starve, and the Huns suffered a heavy stroke from which they never recovered. At the same time a power struggle broke out within their ruling clique, followed by five Khans' declaration of independence and consequent strife among them. The defeated Huhanxie Khan fled south of the Gobi Desert and pledged allegiance to the Han Dynasty.

With a view toward peace among the nations and stability in the north, the Han empire accepted Huhanxie's request by sending troops to protect his state and supplying it with large quantities of grain for the next eight years. In 43 B.C. Huhanxie returned home in the north, but before his departure he formed an alliance with the Han empire, saying "Hans and Huns will be as one family and will not cheat or attack one another from generation to generation." Subsequently the Han empire gave to Huhanxie as his wife a palace maiden, Wang Zhaojun, thereby sealing the peaceful and friendly relations between the Han empire and the Huns.

The peace lasted for about two generations, until the Huns' ruling clique began to split up, about 40 A.D. Youyujianrizhu was made Khan in 48 A.D., backed by his tribesmen. To demonstrate peace with the Han empire he took over the title of his grandfather, Huhanxie, and the next year he sent an envoy to the Han capital to "acknowledge allegiance" to the emperor. He settled inside the Great Wall and set up court in Meiji (now the Dzungarian Banner, or county, in Inner Mongolia), calling his state Southern Hun. Living in the Han empire and gradually adapting to agriculture, the Southern Huns merged after a number of years with the Hans. Meanwhile, many Northern Huns sought

216. Tomb of Wang Zhaojun, near Hohhot. Wang Zhaojun was a palace maiden of the Eastern Han, sent to become the wife of Huhanxie Khan of the Southern Hun

217. Tiger-and-ox golden crown decoration, from a Hun tomb in Hangjin Banner, Inner Mongolia, of the Warring States Period. Diameter 6 3/4″. This luxurious article, with its motifs characteristic of the Huns, illustrates the quality of life among the aristocrats

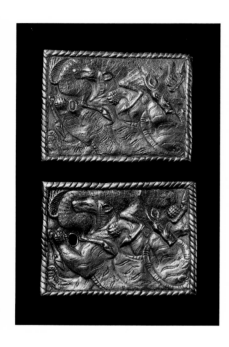

218. Decorative plaque with pattern of tiger attacking a pig. Warring States Period. From a Hun tomb in Buertaohai Commune, Zhungeer Banner. Articles excavated there at the same time bear Chinese seal characters of the Qin period

219. Four tigers attacking an ox, a golden plaque from a Hun tomb in Hangjin Banner. 5 × 3″. The Huns used golden or bronze plaques as the instrument authorizing administrative or military decrees. For an order of great importance a golden plaque was used, which would also serve as a tent decoration, thus showing the prestige and honor of the Khan and his nobility

refuge with the Southern Hun, and a large number of their slaves deserted them. Northern Hun was attacked by the Southern Hun in front, Dingling from the rear, Xianbei from the left, and the various tribes of the Western Region from the right. In 89 A.D. the Han empire began to attack the Northern Huns in Mount Erbujin, Mount Hangai, Hami, and the Altay Mountains. Finally the Khan of the Northern Huns fled with a small number of followers to Kanju (now Samarkand), and the Huns' regime as slaveowners disintegrated. The northern desert they once inhabited came under the Xianbeis, and the Huns, a nation once illustrious in China, disappeared toward the west in the turbulent stream of history.

The Huns were nomadic tribesmen who hunted and grazed their herds and flocks in the wide steppes. The nature of the grasslands, including all animate and inanimate objects, evoked in them their first concepts of beauty. The culture of the Huns was mainly based on the grasslands, and the animals roaming the steppes and forest—sheep, deer, tigers, and horses—formed part of their life and ornamented their articles of daily use. The Huns loved especially to adorn their possessions with tigers. They undoubtedly had to fight the living tiger on occasion, and they were demonstrating their natural bravery in daring to grapple with tigers. The colorful steppe culture of the Huns finds full expression in these excavated relics.

Very early the Huns had learned the use of pottery and bronze through their close contact with the Chinese while they were still in the clan society. But their articles in these materials, such as daggers, were usually small and easy to carry.

The Huns had a spoken, but not a written language. Most of the Hun vocabulary has been preserved by transliteration into the Han language. Mount Chilin, Mount Holan, and Mount Yenzhi are all Hun names still in use today. The Huns called themselves *hu*, meaning westerners. They loved music, and among the best-known *hu* musical instruments were the *hujia*, a reed pipe, and the *pigu*, a military drum. Cai Wenji, a captive for twenty years with the Huns, wrote a long poem entitled *Eighteen Beats of the Hujia*, using the reed pipe rhythm; she noted that the "*hujia* came from the Huns" and "military drums pounded from night till dawn"—apparently there was nightlife among the ancient Huns!

With the contact between the Hans and Huns, particularly

220. Bronze dagger. Warring States Period. From a Hun tomb in Taohongbala, Hangjin Banner

221. Bronze *ho*, wine pot with a long handle. Warring States Period. From a Hun tomb in Waertugou, Yikezhao League. The vessel can be heated directly over a fire, and its small size makes it suitable for use in the yurt

153

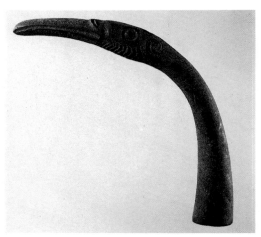

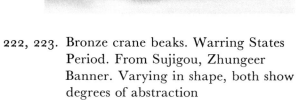

222, 223. Bronze crane beaks. Warring States Period. From Sujigou, Zhungeer Banner. Varying in shape, both show degrees of abstraction

224. Bronze deer with antlers. Warring States Period. From a Hun tomb in Sujigou, Zhungeer Banner. Height 6 1/2″, length 5 3/4″

225. Bronze fawn. Warring States Period. From a Hun tomb in Waertugou, Yikezhao League. The fawn is very tame and lifelike

226. Bronze sheep's head decorating the end of a shaft of a chariot. Warring States Period. From a Hun tomb in Yulongtai, Zhungeer Banner

during the reign of Huhanxie Khan in the period of the Southern Hun, the Huns began to base their culture on peaceful and free interchange instead of on the constant seizure of prisoners for slaves. Large quantities of silks as well as chariots, bronze vessels, swords, armor, flags, and weapons carried by the guard of honor, handicraft articles, and technology were brought into the Hun society. Following the development of farming in areas inhabited by the Huns, well-sinking, city and warehouse construction, and farming techniques also spread among the Huns. On the other hand, their own stockbreeding and steppe culture exerted a corresponding influence on the Han economy. The cattle and horses brought by the Huns in large numbers over the Great Wall improved agriculture and communication in the Central Plain. With the importation of horses and horse-raising techniques, herding in the steppes found a place among the celebrated subjects of ancient Chinese paintings and thus enriched the treasury of human civilization everywhere. The horse-racing and wrestling of the Huns has had some bearing on the pastimes that prevail among the Mongolians and other northern peoples today. All of these occupations can be seen in the murals of Eastern Han unearthed in Inner Mongolia.

Wall Paintings in Horinger

A tomb was excavated in Horinger from the late Eastern Han Dynasty. It was built between 140 and 177 A.D. Some fifty large mural paintings occupy more than 1,000 square feet of the chamber walls. The tomb was for an administrative and military official who had been sent by the central Han government; the paintings show him during his tenure of office, and how he lived in his later years. They also reflect the occupations of the laboring people of different nationalities—grazing, farming, fishing, hunting, and gathering mulberry leaves for silkworms. Ancient cities and towns are depicted, estates, government offices, markets, bridges, and mountain passes, and scenes from daily life such as processions, acrobatic performances, and school recitations.

227. Wall painting from tomb of a governor, sent by the Eastern Han empire to govern in the Wuhuan-inhabited area. Here the governor is seen crossing Juyong Pass on his way to Ningcheng, the Wuhuan center. The Wuhuans, one of the larger tribal groups in the Donghu tribal league (the other being Xianbei), had long been under the control of the Huns. After the Huns were defeated by Eastern Han, a governance was set up in the Wuhuans' area.

228. Herding sheep. Mural from an Eastern Han tomb in Horinger. Depicts the steppes south of the Gobi Desert. Line drawing is used with precision, in a flowing manner

229. An acrobatic show. Mural from an Eastern Han tomb in Horinger

230. Herding the famous Hun horses. Mural from an Eastern Han tomb in Horinger

9. Excavations at Xi'an of the Tang Dynasty

Xi'an, known as Changan in ancient times and one of China's most famous capitals, is today the capital of Shaanxi Province. Located in the center of the central Shaanxi plain and having a mild climate, fertile fields, and facilities for irrigation, the region of Xi'an is well suited for agriculture. In 202 B.C. when Liu Pang had defeated Xiang Yu and founded the Western Han Dynasty, his adviser Zhang Liang persuaded Liu to make Changan his capital, saying, "Guanzhong (central Shaanxi), with Mount Yao and Hangu Pass to the left and Gansu and Sichuan to the right, and surrounded by vast expanses of fertile land and pastures, is a stronghold supported by abundant products."

With its excellent geographical position, Xi'an was the capital of many dynasties—from Western Zhou (11th century B.C.–771 B.C.) to Tang (618–907 A.D.)—for over 2,000 years. Chinese feudal society was at the height of its power and prosperity during the 300 years that Tang made Xi'an its capital. Especially during the reigns of Emperors Tai Zhong (627–649) and Xuan Zhong (713–741), the economy and culture of Tang reached a new peak, and Changan was one of the world's largest metropolises, six times the size of present-day Xi'an (which was built between 1368 and 1398). Although the vicissitudes of history have spared few sites from its early periods, a wealth of cultural objects remained underground. Since 1949 and the founding of New China, Chinese archeologists have undertaken large-scale excavations in Xi'an, bringing to light thousands of cultural objects which illumine China's ancient civilization as never before. Here follows an introduction to the three-colored pottery, gold and silver vessels, and mural paintings of the Tang Dynasty found at Xi'an.

231. Stone lions of the Qian Ling Mausoleum, Xi'an

Three-colored Pottery

Three-colored pottery is a unique form of ceramics, appearing and flourishing in the Tang Dynasty. The clay piece, shaped on a mold, was painted by Tang craftsmen with yellow, green, and brown glazes and fired at temperatures of 1300° to 1400° F.

232. Xi'an, known as Changan in ancient times, was the capital during the Western Han (206 B.C.–24 A.D.) and the Sui to Tang (581–907) dynasties. Large numbers of valuable cultural objects have been excavated. On the left, Xi'an today; the bell tower on the right was built in 1582

233. Dayen (Wild Goose) Pagoda, built in 652 at the suggestion of the famous monk Xuan Zhuang; housed his translations of the Buddhist scriptures he had brought from India. The pagoda has been reconstructed a number of times. Height 210' in 7 stories, square in plan with spiral staircases leading to the top

234. Tombs of emperors dot the surroundings of Xi'an. This is the Qian Ling Mausoleum where Emperor Gao Zhong and Empress Wu Zetian were buried. The large stone sculptures in front of the mausoleum are representative of the art of sculpture in the Tang Dynasty

235. (*opposite*) Three-colored camel. From Tumen, Xi'an. It recalls the caravans on the Silk Road. Height 18 1/2″. Shaanxi Provincial Museum, Xi'an

Tang ceramic wares are distinguished for the gay colors of its glazes. Analysis has shown the chief element of the glaze to be a silicate composed of quartz and minium, or red lead. The coloring agents are metal oxides: powdered iron added to lead glaze fires to yellow, orange, or brown, according to the iron content; different amounts of copper oxide dissolved in lead glaze produce tones from blue to green. These blend and mix in the process of firing, forming special effects and lending variations to the tones.

Apart from making articles of daily use, Tang three-colored pottery was made principally for funerary objects. Among the numerous kinds unearthed in Xi'an, most frequent are warriors, guards of honor, servants, architectural models and rockeries, and animals, including horses and camels. There are also bowls, dishes, ewers, cups, pots, axes, and lampstands, ranging in size from a few inches wide to over three feet high.

The three-colored galloping horse appears unrestrained by his rider, whose seat on his fast-moving mount demonstrates his skilled horsemanship. His robe is painted with blue glaze, which

236. Three-colored galloping horse and rider. Excavated in the outskirts of Xi'an. Height about 9 3/4″. The rider's robe is painted with blue glaze, making this a rare piece among three-colored Tang pottery. Collection the Municipal Cultural Administration Council, Xi'an

237. Three-colored seated woman.
Excavated in Wangjiawen, Xi'an. It
portrays a Tang woman in elegant
dress. Height 18 1/2″. Shaanxi
Provincial Museum, Xi'an

238. (*opposite*) Three-colored *Musicians
and Dancer on Camelback*. Excavated
in Princess Yong Tai's tomb. Height
19″. A rare work of art, it shows a
band of musicians and a dancer
performing on the back of a camel.
Shaanxi Provincial Museum, Xi'an

239, 240. Three three-colored women.
Excavated in Hojia, outskirts of Xi'an.
Collection Chinese Museum of
History, Beijing

puts the work in the class known as "three colors plus blue"; the form is very rare and therefore much valued among pieces of three-colored pottery. The three-colored seated woman shows a dressed-up Tang woman who is smiling faintly and looks lively and amiable. She is attired in a close-fitting sleeveless chemise and a gaily patterned skirt that falls to the ground; her hair is tied back in a tall chignon. She would be considered fashionably dressed at any time.

A most entertaining example of three-colored pottery is the *Musicians and Dancer on Camelback*. The camel raises its head and brays as the five musicians on his back, each in distinctive pose, are absorbed in playing their instruments. We can almost hear the sound and rhythm of their music. Three-colored Tang pottery wares are more than works of art in their own right; with the rich flavor of their subject matter, they reflect many aspects of social life and offer valuable material for the study of Tang society.

241. Three-colored camel with rider. Excavated in Zheng Rentai's tomb, Tang Dynasty. Height 20". This piece is rather rare among pottery camels because the rider is a "non-Han," with high-bridged nose and deep-set eyes. In Chinese history, "non-Han" generally refers to people living in the vast area of present-day Xinjiang, and further west. Zhao Ling Museum

242. Three-colored rockery and pond. Excavated in Zhongpao on the outskirts of Xi'an. Height 7". A rare piece for its original conception and fine workmanship. Shaanxi Provincial Museum, Xi'an

243. Three-colored lion biting its hind paw. Excavated in Wangjiawen, Xi'an. Height 7 3/4". Shaanxi Provincial Museum, Xi'an

244. Three-colored flask, the mouth in the shape of a cock's head. Shows influence of Persian style. Height 12 1/2". Shaanxi Provincial Museum, Xi'an

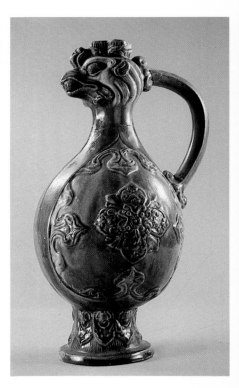

245. Three-colored horses. Excavated in Princess Yong Tai's tomb. Tang craftsmen portrayed the form and spirit of horses through careful observation and great artistry. Shaanxi Provincial Museum, Xi'an

246. Three-colored non-Han in the pose of leading a horse. Excavated in Princess Yong Tai's tomb. Height 6″. Shaanxi Provincial Museum, Xian

247. Bowl in solid gold, carved with animal, bird, and flower patterns. Excavated in Hojia, outskirts of Xi'an. The background is decorated with glittering fish eggs. Height 2″, diameter 5″. Shaanxi Provincial Museum, Xi'an

Gold and Silver Vessels

Many gold and silver vessels were unearthed around Xi'an, especially in two extraordinary caches discovered in 1970 at Hojia, a village south of the city. Among the more than 1,000 objects, 270 were vessels of gold and silver, unprecedented for their variety, workmanship, and quality of preservation.

Archeologists working with historical records and with on-the-spot data have determined that the caches were located on the site of the residence of Prince Fen. The hidden objects perhaps belonged to the prince, and might have been buried to save them from the flames of war during the rebellion of An Lushan, the mid-eighth-century viceroy, in the cities of Pinglu, Fanyang, and Hodong, and then overlooked in the protracted chaos. The caches include bowls, dishes, saucers, pots, pans, boxes, and stoves. In technique, according to experts, the works are complicated and refined: cutting, polishing, soldering, riveting, and plating were all commonly used. Articles such as bowls, dishes, and boxes show marks of cutting, with clear, fine, concentric whorls. The clasp of the lock was processed to fasten tightly. The axis of the pieces rarely varies, an indication that simple lathes were already in use and that the art of cutting was mature. The technique of soldering was also at a high level, for the solder marks are straight and the seams almost invisible.

In their decorative patterns the gold and silver vessels are elegant, even elaborate. Tang craftsmen skillfully blended the traditional dragon, tiger, finch, and cloud motifs with imported grape and lotus designs, as well as symmetrical flowers and animals, to form rich designs. These are laid out so that order is united with a degree of variation. Each design contains different flowers and animals, all of exquisite workmanship. The golden bowl, for example, is carved with birds, animals, and flowers, and the background is filled with glittering fish eggs. Some silver vessels have gilded motifs in a special effect of high relief.

Among the excavated articles is a silver jar shaped like a wineskin, on either side of which was hammered out a horse, plated with gold, its neck tied with a waving scarf. The horse seems to be dancing, with its forelegs straight, hind legs bent, and tail raised, and it holds a cup in its mouth. According to historical records, "Emperor Xuan Zhong once ordered 400 horses to be trained to dance." Many Tang poems mention dancing horses, and the example on this silver jar may well be one of these.

248. Silver jar in the shape of a wineskin. Excavated in Hojia, outskirts of Xi'an. Each side is decorated with a dancing horse holding a golden cup in its mouth. Height 7″. Shaanxi Provincial Museum, Xi'an

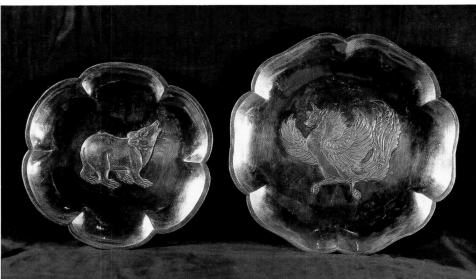

249. Silver trays carved with gilded animals. Excavated in Hojia, outskirts of Xi'an. Diameters 6″ and 4 3/4″. Shaanxi Provincial Museum, Xi'an

169

250. Silver tray shaped like an opened peach, with carved gilded foxes. Excavated in Hojia, outskirts of Xi'an. Diameter 5″. Shaanxi Provincial Museum, Xi'an

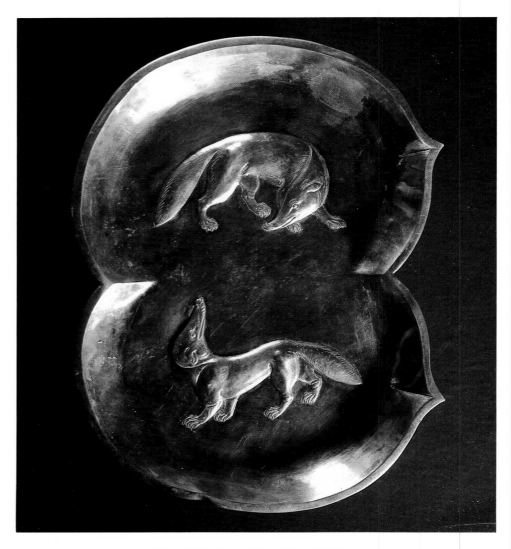

251. Golden lock and key. Excavated in Hojia, outskirts of Xi'an. Length 5 1/2″. Shaanxi Provincial Museum, Xi'an

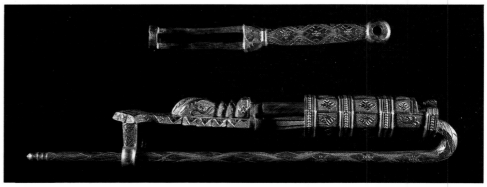

252. Carved golden boxes. Excavated in Hojia, outskirts of Xi'an. Diameters 2″ and 1 1/2″. Shaanxi Provincial Museum, Xi'an

253. Octagonal gilded cup. It is in the Persian Sassanian style. Excavated in Hojia, outskirts of Xi'an. Height 2". Shaanxi Provincial Museum, Xi'an

254. Silver jar carved with gilded parrot pattern. Excavated in Hojia, outskirts of Xi'an. Height 9 1/2". Shaanxi Provincial Museum, Xi'an

Murals

Since 1949 large numbers of wall paintings have been unearthed in Tang tombs in Xi'an and the surrounding area. The tombs of Princess Yong Tai and of the Princes Zhang Huai and Yi De, in the Qian Ling Mausoleum of Emperor Gao Zhong and Empress Wu Zetian on Mount Liangshan, have yielded the greatest number of a high artistic value.

Prince Zhang Huai, second son of Emperor Gao Zhong, had been made crown prince, but was demoted to a commoner in 680 for opposing his mother, Wu Zetian. He died in Bazhou (now Bazhong County, Sichuan) in 684. When the succeeding Emperor Zhong Zhong was enthroned, he had Prince Zhang Huai's coffin moved to the Qian Ling Mausoleum and buried as Prince Yong; in 711, posthumously, the title of Prince Zhang Huai was conferred on Prince Yong.

The passage leading to Prince Zhang Huai's tomb is 233 feet long, and over fifty groups of painted figures extend on both sides for more than 4,300 square feet. *The Hunt*, a masterpiece of Tang Dynasty mural painting, depicts some fifty horsemen and camels, hawks, hounds, and cheetahs; it stretches forty feet along the wall of the passage. Led by a rider holding a banner with a bear's head and escorted by dozens of riders, a man dressed in a purplish-gray robe jogs along leisurely on a white horse, followed by a mounted guard. Among the trees at a distance run camels bearing heavy packs.

The picture imparts a strong sense of movement. Hunting is a common theme in ancient Chinese painting, but this example is distinguished by its magnificent scale. The mural illustrates the Tang painters' developed technique. The drawing of the figures is accurate and unified, reflecting their expressive mien and inner thoughts. Horses are prominent in painting, an indication of their importance as a means of transport.

Murals have a long history in Chinese art, but they attain a

259. *Captain of the Guard*

high point of excellence in the Tang Dynasty. Celebrated painters such as Yen Liben, Wu Taozi, Li Sixun, and Wang Wei produced a number of murals: Wu Taozi painted over four hundred murals on monastery walls in Changan and Luoyang. On the order of Emperor Xuan Zhong, the artist executed in one day a giant mural on the wall of Da Tong Hall of Xing Qing Palace, depicting the vast land traversed by the Jialing River. Perhaps the most brilliant works of the Tang master painters do not survive today, but a glimpse of their art is provided by these wall paintings that had lain dormant underground for more than a thousand years.

East-West Cultural Exchanges During the Tang Dynasty

Changan in the Tang Dynasty was the political, economic, and cultural center of China. It was a cosmopolitan city of over a million people. The Silk Road that linked Europe with Asia in ancient times started from Changan, passed along the Hexi Corridor and across the Tarim Basin, traversed the high Pamir Mountains, and eventually reached the countries bordering the Mediterranean Sea. Opened as early as during the Western Han, this east-west route of land communication flourished as never before during the Tang Dynasty, which adopted an open policy, established friendly relations with over three hundred countries connected with this artery of communication, and made its influence widely felt. Overseas Chinese communities are still known today as Tang Ren Jie ("street of the Tang people").

Silk was transported and marketed in bulk in Central Asia and Western Asia during the Tang Dynasty, and some found its way through the Persian Gulf to Rome and beyond. According to ancient records, the exchange of horses for silk in some western countries was at the rate of one good horse to forty bolts of silk

173

brocade; when hundreds or even a thousand horses were sent east, the transaction fetched an enormous quantity of silk. The three-colored pottery camels fully laden with this precious cargo recall those people who traveled on the long Silk Road, crossing deserts and icy peaks to promote trade and cultural exchange. Among the pottery figures that have been excavated, many have faces with Central Asian, West Asian, North African, or European features, showing China's understanding of the west and the frequency of east-west contacts. Many foreigners also came to Changan, where they were received in such establishments as the Hong Lu Si temple and Li Bin Yuan hostel, both set up by the government. Among the foreign visitors were envoys, craftsmen, merchants, and artists, who brought with them western culture, science, and technique. Tang was able to create a flourishing feudal culture because it constantly assimilated fresh elements from abroad. The three-colored flask in the shape of a cock's head and the elephant-head drinking horn found in Xi'an drew their patterns from those on vessels of gold and silver of the Sassanian Empire of Persia. The bead-edged octagonal gilded cup with musicians and dancers in relief shows unmistakable knowledge of Persian style. The crystal cup, glass bowl, and gold-inlaid ox-headed cup excavated at the same time may well have come directly from Persia and Arabia. Among the cached objects were found an East Roman gold coin and a Persian silver coin, both evidence of the east-west trade.

The *Musicians and Dancer on Camelback* also reflects cultural exchange between east and west. Three of the figures look like Central or Western Asians, with high-bridged noses, deep-set eyes, and curly hair. Two other figures are Han in appearance. During the Tang Dynasty, music and dances from Central, West, and South Asia became very popular in Changan. The ten-part music described as performed in the Tang court must indeed have absorbed the essence of this foreign music.

The *Polo Players* in the murals in Prince Zhang Huai's tomb shows many riders, five wielding mallets as they chase the ball in the fashionable court pastime imported from Persia. The sport, played on horseback, was widely popular among the nobles—all the Tang emperors after Xuan Zhong loved to play polo. A carved stone tablet found in 1956 at the site of Han Guan Hall in Da Ming Palace reads: "Han Guan Hall and polo court, built in the month of Yi Mo of the Year of Xin Hai in the Reign of Da Ho of the Great Tang." The mention of the polo field in connection with the construction of the palace shows how greatly esteemed the sport was at that time.

260. *Polo Players* (detail). Entire dimensions 75 × 69″. Shaanxi Provincial Museum, Xi'an

10. Silk, Paintings, and Figurines from Turpan on the Silk Road

Visitors always admire the gorgeous silk fabrics displayed in the Museum of the Xinjiang Uygur Autonomous Region at Ürümqi. Most of these come from the hot, dry region of Turpan.

Turpan: A Strategic Point

Turpan is a depressed basin, the lowest point of the Asian continent, 150 feet below sea level, near the Tianshan range. Turpan County with its many oases lies in the center. The land is hot and dry, but irrigation is well developed and the soil is fertile. It has been a land of plenty since ancient times, known far and wide for its grapes and cotton. During the 1,000 years from the Western Han (206 B.C.–24 A.D.) to the Tang (618–907) dynasties, the county town of Turpan was continuously of strategic importance.

The ancient name for Turpan, Qoco, appears for the first time in the *Chronicles of the Han Dynasty*. In 62 B.C. the Han Emperor Xuan Di sent 300 troops to Qoco to open up the land. It became thereafter a stronghold of the Han Dynasty in the Western Region. During the Eastern Jin Dynasty (317–420) it came under the jurisdiction of the State of Qianliang, and was known after 327 as the Qoco prefecture; independence under a feudal regime came after the fifth century, with the Qu family having the longest rule, 141 years. The first ruler, Qu Jia, came from Gansu. By the Tang Dynasty, Qoco's ruler, Qu Wentai, often detained and looted the Tang emissaries who asked permission to pass through Qoco. To maintain unity in China and to keep traffic moving along the Silk Road, Emperor Tai Zhong (627–649) sent troops to overthrow the Qu Dynasty. They succeeded, and Qoco became known as Xichang, later as Xizhou, and in the mid-seventh century a Governor's Office was set up at Yarkhoto of Qoco. (Later this was moved to Kucha, in present-day Kuche County.) The Governor's Office was the supreme military and administrative unit acting for the Tang court in the Western Region. It exercised jurisdiction over the entire territory of present-day Xinjiang, and the vast areas east and south of Balkhash Lake (in present-day Kazakh S.S.R.). By that time the Silk

262. Turpan was known as Qoco in ancient times. It was on the northern route of the Silk Road during the thousand years between the Western Han (206 B.C.–24 A.D.) and the Tang (618–907) dynasties

All works illustrated in this chapter are in the Museum of the Xinjiang Uygur Autonomous Region, Ürümqi

261. (*opposite*) Tang brocade from Astana. The motifs of elephants, lions, and cattle are from Central and West Asian art

Road was a most prosperous artery. Supported by this east-west commerce, Qoco's economy and culture developed rapidly as successive caravans passed through it the whole year round. It was the main commercial center west of Dunhuang. The remains of the ancient city are still to be seen in the Flame Hill People's Commune, twenty-five miles southeast of the county town of Turpan. The circumference of Qoco city is three miles, with a city wall made out of clay rammed solid. After a thousand years of erosion, the remaining part still stands thirty-six feet high. Nothing remains intact inside the city, but the ruins suggest a once prosperous urban life. Qoco was abandoned in the fourteenth century, toward the end of the Yuan Dynasty, some 700 years ago.

Fine Silk Fabrics

Outside Qoco there are two small villages, Astana and Kara-khoja, and in the desert between them is a group of ancient tombs. Since the founding of New China, Chinese archeologists have conducted thirteen campaigns in some four hundred tombs, bringing to light a great number of relics. Among these are silk fabrics unparalleled in quantity and variety, well preserved by the extremely dry climate.

Finely made plain silk was discovered in the tombs belonging to the Northern Dynasties (fourth to sixth centuries A.D.). Some specimens have woven tree designs in crimson, sapphire blue, green, light yellow, and white; and animal designs in brown, green, white, yellow, and blue. The colors are varied and the

263. Brocade with trees, of the 6th century, from Astana, Turpan
264. Brocade with paired lambs, trees, and chickens, of the Northern Dynasties (5th to 6th centuries), from Astana, Turpan

265. Brocade with birds and horned animals of the State of Beiliang (4th and 5th centuries), unearthed at Astana, Turpan
266. Brocade with the Chinese characters *hu wang* of the Northern Dynasties (5th to 6th centuries), from Astana, Turpan
267. Printed gauze of the Tang Dynasty, from Astana, Turpan
268. Tang tapestry with birds and flowers, from Astana, Turpan. Made of silk in eight bright colors. The sophisticated design is minutely executed, a rare specimen of Tang weaving

265

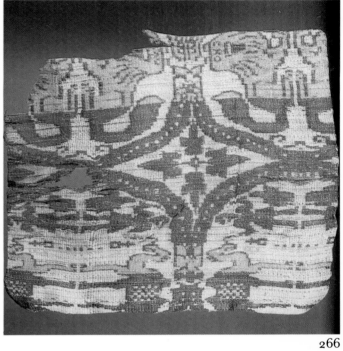

266

268

267

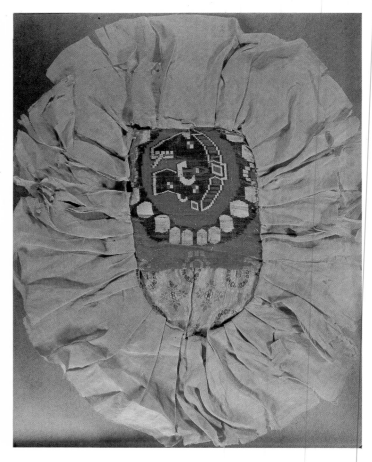

269. Silk shoes of the Eastern Jin Dynasty (317–420), from Astana, Turpan. They bear Han characters meaning "rich and noble" and "for marquis and prince"

270. Cloud-pattern silk shoes. Length 11″ They are made of three different pieces of brocade, and are in good condition.

271. A brocade veil with bear's head and forepaws, of the Tang Dynasty, from Astana, Turpan. It covered the face of the deceased

patterns well executed. The fine and thin fabric is an improvement on the earlier examples from the Eastern Han Period.

Inside the sixth- and seventh-century tombs were found silks woven in western patterns. The designs are arranged in rows like that of Han brocade, but the motifs are Central Asian or West Asian, such as cattle, lions, and elephants. Some of the patterns are peculiar to the contemporary Sassanian Empire of Persia: a pair of birds or a pair of animals within a string of beads. Possibly these were made for export. Persian silver and East Roman gold coins were found with the fabrics, evidence of the east-west trade.

A new level in both craftsmanship and design is reached in the Tang fabrics, especially the brocades. The piece of brocade illustrated here has flowers, birds, trees, and rocks, in eight colors on a red background. The composition is sophisticated and well knit, vivid and colorful. Found with this piece of silk was a pair of silk shoes with cloud patterns, made of three different kinds of brocade.

Ancient Documents

The Astana-Karakhoja tombs contained thousands of documents which had been used as material for making shoes, hats, sashes, pillows, and mattresses for the dead. The documents are badly damaged, but the characters on them are clear to see. They are contracts, accounts, official documents, private letters, and copies of classical literature, and they reflect political, economic, cultural, and military affairs.

Turpan's economy was quite an advanced one. The grain crops mentioned in the documents are wheat, barley, millet, and broomcorn millet; the industrial crops are cotton, mulberry trees, beans, and flax. Cotton was planted in Turpan about the fifth century. The earliest species planted in Turpan was the

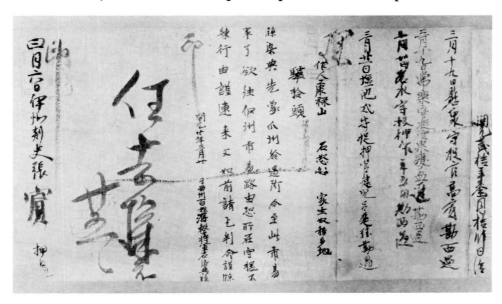

272. A travel permit of the Tang Dynasty, from Astana, Turpan

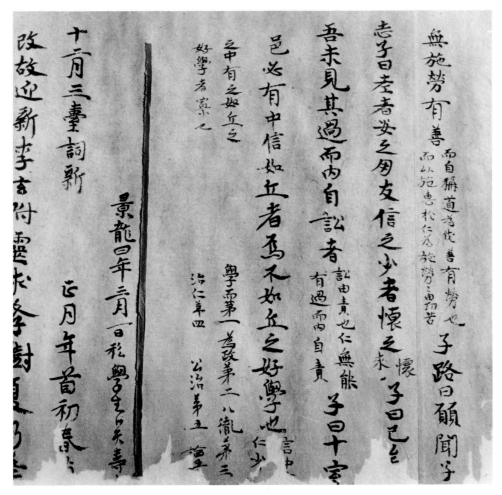

273. Remnants of a copy of *The Analects With Annotations by Zheng Xuan*, the fourth year (710) of the reign of Emperor Zhong Zhong of the Tang Dynasty. *The Analects* is a Confucian classic, with annotations by the famous Han Dynasty scholar Zheng Xuan. During the Han Dynasty, the book was a primer for children

274. *Girl Dancer*, a Tang silk painting from Astana, Turpan. 18 × 8 1/2″

levant cotton from Africa, probably introduced via the Silk Road.

Turpan has good grapes today, and people were already planting them centuries ago. Records of grape cultivation and wine-making have been found: one, dated 422 A.D., lists under the disbursement items that seven *hu* of wine were paid out on the 4th day of the 11th month. Under the Qu regime, Qoco collected as tax a great amount of wine from the vineyards, 973 *hu* in one instance. Evidently the cultivation of grapes and the making of wine were well under way.

As a stopover for the east-west traffic, Turpan did a brisk business in ancient times. An account of commissions collected at an official market during the Qu Dynasty records items of transaction that include gold and silver, sal ammoniac, spices, medicinal herbs, and silk. One customer bought 50 pounds of silk and 10 ounces of gold, another 572 pounds of spices. None of the buyers or sellers was Chinese. The commodities may have been shipped from outside or produced locally.

Travel permits occur among the documents. By the Tang Dynasty the travel permit had become part of a regular security system. Permits had to be shown at outposts, and the date and destination registered and signed by the garrison officer. Travel-

275. Sketch showing reconstruction of original composition of *Ladies at a Game of Chess*.

276. *Ladies at a Game of Chess*, two boys. Height 23″

277. Central portion of a Tang silk painting, *Ladies at a Game of Chess*, from Tomb 187, Astana, Turpan. The lady on the left is missing. Height 24 3/4″

278. *Ladies at a Game of Chess*, figures at right

ing without a permit or with a false permit was punished. The permit illustrated here is under the name of Shi Randian, a merchant going from Xizhou (Turpan) to Yizhou (Hami) on business.

The literary classics discovered in the tombs consist mainly of remnants of Confucius's *The Analects, with Annotations by Zheng Xuan.* At the end is an inscription written by the copyist in 710, the 4th year of the reign of Zhong Zhong of the Tang, that says, "Disciple Bu Tianshou of Ningchang Town, Qoco County, Xizhou, at the age of 12." Confucianism had been protected since the rulers of the Han Dynasty, and Zheng Xuan was a famous Han scholar. *The Analects* was used as a children's primer, and the presence of this copy indicates that culture and education were about the same in Qoco as in the rest of the country.

Silk Paintings

A number of paintings on silk were found in the Tang tombs at Astana. The *Girl Dancer* is wonderfully preserved. She is pretty and graceful; she wears a yellow and blue blouse open at the neck, and a long skirt trailing to the floor. She has a silk shawl over her left shoulder, with one end tucked in at her bosom. The right hand is missing, but to judge from the sleeve, she was raising that arm in a dancing movement. It is a pity that of another painting of a girl playing an instrument, only half the skirt and one shoe remain.

Ladies at a Game of Chess from Tomb 187 is worthy of special note. It was found in pieces, but through repair the figures of eleven women and children have reappeared. Archeologists have restored the original composition by studying the relations

280. (*opposite*) Clay horse with decorative harness and saddle. Tang Dynasty. Height 30″

281. Colored clay figure of a Tang lady on horseback. She wears a low-necked blouse, long gown, large hat, and veil, perhaps the traveling costume of the day. Height 15 1/2″

282. A Tang warrior on horseback, painted in color, from Astana, Turpan. Height 14″

283. Girl dancers from Tomb 206, Astana, Turpan. The tomb belongs to General Zhang Xiong of Qoco and his wife. The heads are clay, the bodies wood, and the arms paper; the dresses are made of silk. The face is carefully painted with eyes and eyebrows, and there are ornaments in the hair. This kind of figurine has never been discovered elsewhere

284. Clay figurines of women working, Tang Dynasty, Xizhou region. Heights 3″ to 6″

285. A Tang eunuch, with clay head and wooden body. Astana, Turpan. Height 13 1/2″

286. A clay polo player on horseback, from Astana, Turpan. Height 14 1/2″

279. Pastries excavated from a Tang tomb, Astana, Turpan. Diameters 1 1/2 to 2″

among the figures and the objects in the foreground area, and the traces of trees. In the center of the picture there were originally two women playing chess. The one on the right is putting a piece on the board with her slender fingers; her partner on the left is missing. Behind the player is a woman holding a cup of tea, and a group of women and maidservants watching the game. Behind the missing player the greater part of two maids has been preserved; one is about to select a chesspiece from the pot, and the other is holding a piece in her left hand and seems to be watching the progress of the game. In the distance women and maids are looking after two boys playing in the woods. The painting is badly damaged, yet enough remains to tell us something of what Xizhou had attained in the arts during the Tang Dynasty. The traditional pictorial style had been carried on and developed. The lines are concise and flowing, but full of variations; the color is simple and bright; the shading technique gives a feeling of three dimensions.

Clay and Wooden Figurines

Most of the figurines are made of wood and clay. In one type the wooden horses and grooms are carved in separate parts and then put together before being painted. Another type has a head of clay, a rectangular body of wood, and arms of paper, and is dressed in silk. The faces are beautifully painted, with eyes and eyebrows, and ornaments in the hair; figurines of this type have never been found anywhere else. The women figurines seen here wear blouses and long skirts to the ground. On their foreheads are beautiful ornaments, and their hair is dressed in high rolls.

280

281

282

283

284

285

286

Shawls drape over the shoulders; their dresses are more or less like the dancing girl in the silk painting. This must have been the fashion in the Xizhou region, and it is similar to that of the three-colored pottery lady of the Tang Dynasty unearthed in Xi'an (see Chapter 9).

The clay figures are brightly painted. In one group, women are reenacting their daily activities—winnowing grain, pounding rice, grinding grain, kneading dough, and baking cakes. A eunuch is cleverly made to express fully his obsequious, yet bullying nature. There is also a polo player. Swinging a curved stick, he is about to strike the ball from horseback. The game originated in Persia, and was introduced into Changan during the Tang Dynasty; this clay player testifies that polo came to China by the Silk Road.

Map

Chronology

Index

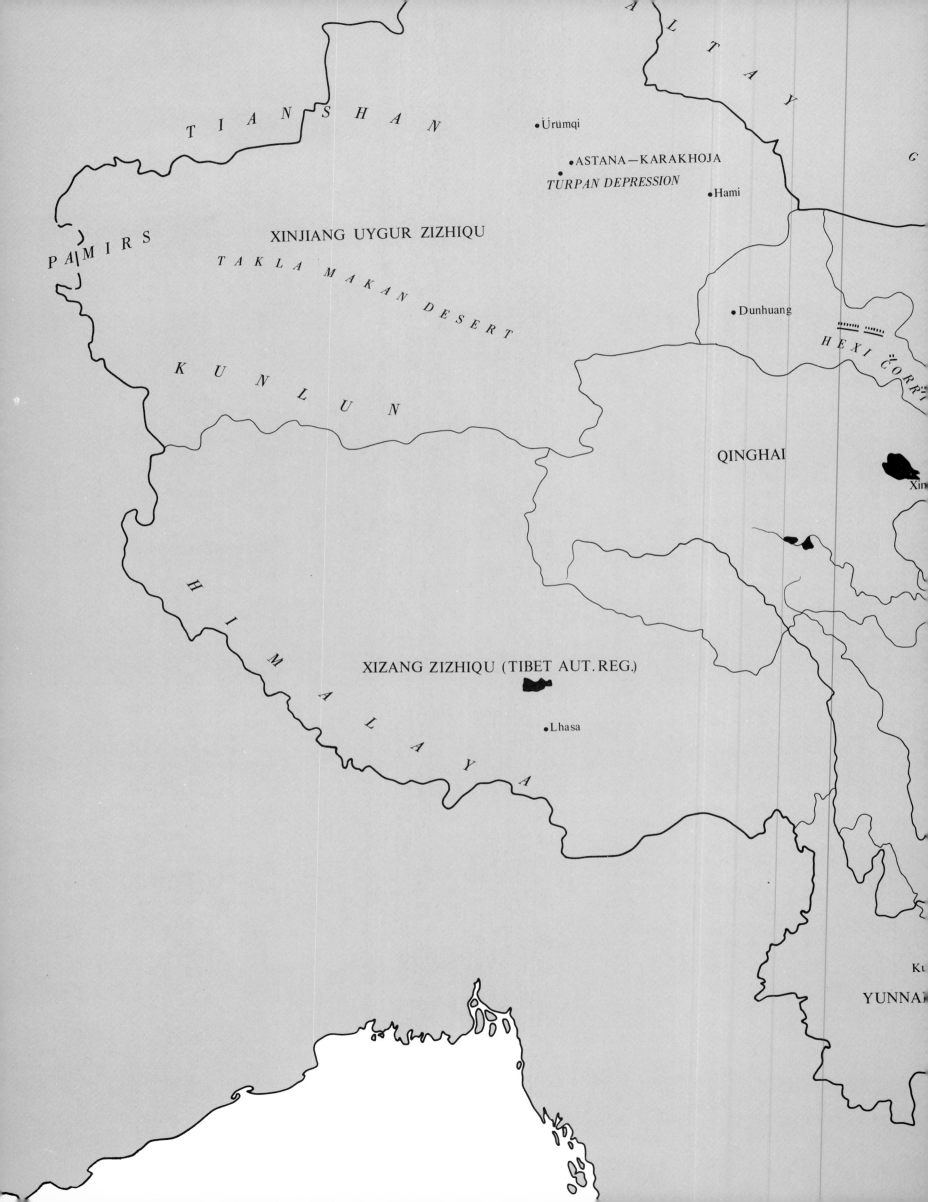

Chronology

Xia (Hsia) Dynasty	21st–16th century B.C.
Shang Dynasty	16th–11th century B.C.
Zhou (Chou) Dynasty	1122 B.C.–256 B.C.
Western Zhou	1122 B.C.–771 B.C.
Eastern Zhou	770 B.C.–256 B.C.
Spring and Autumn Period	727 B.C.–481 B.C.
Warring States Period	475 B.C.–221 B.C.
Qin (Chin) Dynasty	221 B.C.–206 B.C.
Han Dynasty	206 B.C.–220 A.D.
Western Han	206 B.C.–24 A.D.
Eastern Han	25 A.D.–220 A.D.
The Three Kingdoms	220–265
Wei Dynasty	220–265
Shu (Shu-han) Dynasty	221–263
Wu Dynasty	222–280
Jin (Tsin) Dynasty	265–420
Western Jin	265–316
Eastern Jin	317–420
Southern and Northern Dynasties	386–589
Southern Dynasties	420–589
Song (Sung)	420–479

Qi (Ch'i)		479–502
Liang		502–557
Chen		557–589
Northern Dynasties	386–581	
Bei Wei (Northern Wei)		386–534
Dong Wei (Eastern Wei)		534–550
Bei Qi (Northern Chi)		550–577
Xi Wei (Western Wei)		535–557
Bei Zhou (Northern Chou)		557–581
Sui Dynasty	581–618	
Tang Dynasty	618–907	
Five Dynasties	907–960	
Song (Sung) Dynasty	960–1279	
Bei Song (Northern Sung)		960–1127
Nan Song (Southern Sung)		1127–1279
Liao Dynasty (Manchuria)	907–1142	
Xi Xia (Western Hsia) Dynasty	1032–1227	
Jin (Tsin) Dynasty	1115–1234	
Yuan (Yüan) Dynasty	1206–1368	
Ming Dynasty	1368–1644	
Qing (Ching) Dynasty	1644–1911	

Index

A

B

D

E

F

Z

Photographic Credits

The publishers wish to thank the following institutions for permitting the reproduction of photographs in their possession: Chapter 1: Archeological Institute, Beijing; Chapter 2: Cultural Relics Department, Hebei Province, Shijiazhuang; Chapter 3: Hubei Provincial Museum, Wuhan; Chapter 5: Hunan Provincial Museum, Changsha.

The following photographers have supplied the majority of photographs reproduced in this book, and their courtesy is gratefully acknowledged:

Chapter 1: Chen Heyi, He Shiyao, Li Zisheng, Qian Hao, Wang Lu, Wei Dezhong
Chapter 2: Wang Lu
Chapter 3: Gao Mingyi, Luo Wenfa, Sun Zhijiang
Chapter 4: Huang Taopeng, Li Miao
Chapter 5: Ao Enhong, Sun Zhijiang, Wang Lu
Chapter 6: Ru Suichu
Chapter 7: Cai Yixuan, Huang Taopeng, Yue Banghu
Chapter 8: Li Miao, Luo Wenfa
Chapter 9: Ru Suichu
Chapter 10: Ru Suichu, Wang Lu